To: Ann

The woman who [told?]
me that giving up is not
an option.

T... ...ary 2025

Life Skills for Young Adults

The Guide Every Young Adult Needs! To Rise Above Life's Challenges, Achieve Financial Security, Become Emotionally Resilient and Enjoy Career Success

SquareRoets

One MA done — thanks Ann
One book written — and watch
this space for the rest.
Lots of Love
Ilse.

© Copyright SquareRoets 2024 - All rights reserved.

The content within this book may not be reproduced, duplicated, or transmitted without direct written permission from the author or the publisher.

Under no circumstances will any blame or legal responsibility be held against the publisher or author for any damages, reparation, or monetary loss due to the information contained within this book. Either directly or indirectly. You are responsible for your own choices, actions, and results.

Legal Notice:

This book is copyright-protected. This book is only for personal use. You cannot amend, distribute, sell, use, quote, or paraphrase any part of this book's content without the author's or publisher's consent.

Disclaimer Notice:

Please note the information contained within this document is for educational and entertainment purposes only. All effort has been expended to present accurate, up-to-date, reliable, and complete information. No warranties of any kind are declared or implied. Readers acknowledge that the author does not render legal, financial, medical, or professional advice. The content within this book has been derived from various sources. Please consult a licensed professional before attempting any techniques outlined in this book.

By reading this document, the reader agrees that under no circumstances is the author responsible for any losses, direct or indirect, which are incurred as a result of the use of the information contained within this document, including, but not limited to, — errors, omissions, or inaccuracies.

Contents

Introduction	7
1. UNLEASHING YOUR FINANCIAL SUPERPOWERS	11
Crafting Your First Budget: A Step-by-Step Guide	12
Understanding Credit Scores and How to Build Yours	14
Saving Strategies for Short-Term Goals: Tips and Tricks	16
Basic Investing for Beginners: Where to Start	18
Smart Spending: How to Evaluate Needs vs. Wants	21
Navigating Student Loans: Payment Plans and Forgiveness Programs	23
2. ACHIEVING FINANCIAL INDEPENDENCE	27
Side Hustles: Turning Passions into Profits	28
Negotiating Your First Salary: Do's and Don'ts	30
Essential Insurance Policies for Young Adults	32
Planning for Retirement in Your 20s: A Beginner's Guide	35
The Art of Frugal Living Without Sacrificing Joy	37
Financial Health Check-ups: Quarterly Review Best Practices	40
3. BUILDING EMOTIONAL STRENGTH	45
Identifying and Managing Stress Triggers	46
The Power of Mindfulness: Techniques for Relieving Anxiety	49
Overcoming Fear of Failure: Lessons in Resilience	51
Developing a Positive Self-Image in the Social Media Age	54

    Navigating Grief and Loss as a Young Adult   56
    Cultivating Joy: Practical Steps to Increase Happiness   59

4. FOSTERING HEALTHY RELATIONSHIPS   63
    Effective Communication: Beyond Words   64
    Setting Boundaries: The Foundation for Healthy Relationships   66
    Dealing with Conflict: Strategies for Resolution   68
    Building Strong Friendships in Adulthood   71
    Romantic Relationships: Red Flags and Compatibility   73
    Networking: Creating Valuable Professional Relationships   76

5. PATHWAYS TO PROFESSIONAL FULFILMENT   83
    Discovering Your Passion: Self-Assessment Tools   84
    Exploring Career Paths: Interviews with Professionals   87
    The Role of Internships: Gaining Real-World Experience   89
    Crafting a Winning Resume and Cover Letter   92
    Ace the Interview: Techniques and Tips   95
    Navigating Your First Job: Expectations vs Reality   98

6. SKILLS FOR THE MODERN WORKPLACE   103
    Digital Literacy: Navigating Today's Tech-Driven World   104
    Time Management: Tools and Techniques for Efficiency   106
    The Importance of Emotional Intelligence at Work   109
    Creative Problem-Solving and Innovation   112
    Leadership Skills for the Emerging Professional   115
    The Basics of Project Management   119

7. MASTERING DAILY LIFE TASKS — 123

   Cooking Basics: Quick, Healthy Meals on a Budget — 124

   Keeping It Clean: Simplified Housekeeping Strategies — 126

   Laundry 101: From Sorting to Stain Removal — 128

   Basic Home Repairs: A DIY Guide — 131

   Car Maintenance: Essentials Every Young Adult Should Know — 134

   Personal Safety: Awareness and Self-Defense Basics — 136

8. NAVIGATING THE DIGITAL WORLD — 141

   Managing Your Digital Footprint: Privacy and Safety Online — 142

   Social Media Smarts: Building Your Brand Positively — 144

   Understanding Global Issues: Becoming a Global Citizen — 146

   Traveling Smart: Tips for Safe and Budget-Friendly Adventures — 149

   Volunteering: Giving Back and Gaining Experience — 151

   Continuous Learning: Keeping Skills Updated in a Rapidly Changing World — 154

   Conclusion — 161

   References — 165

Introduction

"The future belongs to those who believe in the beauty of their dreams."

— Eleanor Roosevelt

If you were asked: "What does it mean to be 'ready' for the real world?" how would you answer? If you really think about it, academic achievements are important, but you also need practical skills to function successfully as an adult. Unfortunately, practical skills are seldom taught in schools, and although many parents impart basic skills to their children, such as preparing a meal or changing a car's tire, they need to teach them about completing a tax return or understanding a complex financial statement.

This book was born from a need to bridge that gap. I aim to offer you a roadmap—a blend of mentorship, guidance, and actionable knowledge—to confidently tackle the transition into adulthood. Whether you are stepping out of high school into college or from academia into the workforce, this guide and my mentorship will ensure you aren't just surviving but thriving.

With over 30 years of teaching experience and a deep dive into the teenage brain through various courses, including an impactful NLP coaching certification, I've tailored this guide with a keen understanding of what young adults face today. This guide isn't just professional insight; it's a personal journey of learning and unlearning I've walked and now share with you.

You might be a young adult seeking direction, a parent eager to equip your child for life beyond school, or an educator looking to supplement traditional education with core life skills. Whomever you are, you'll find this book useful. It's designed to empower you with practical advice directly applicable to your unique experiences and challenges.

This guide tackles key areas such as achieving financial security without drowning in jargon, building emotional resilience in adversity, and carving out a successful career path with realistic expectations. It's structured to walk you through each facet of adulthood—from managing your finances and understanding emotional intelligence to navigating career choices.

As we embark on this journey together, expect a blend of practical step-by-step instructions, relatable personal anecdotes, and easy-to-understand strategies that cater to the needs of a diverse audience. It's inclusive, straightforward, and, most importantly, practical.

By the end of this book, you will not only be prepared for the so-called "real world" but also inspired to shape it, armed with the confidence and clarity you need to overcome life's myriad challenges.

1
Unleashing Your Financial Superpowers

"Do not save what is left after spending, but spend what is left after saving."

— Warren Buffett

Have you ever found yourself wondering where your money vanished? You're not alone. Learning to manage finances should begin with your first allowance or the money you earn doing odd jobs for neighbors. You suddenly have money of your own to do with as you please. Ideally, you should be already taught to save a portion, perhaps in a piggy bank. Many young adults are thrust into financial independence when they secure their first job. Whether you still live in your parent's home or an apartment alone or with friends, you need to pay rent. The first step is to craft a budget to understand where your money is spent each month; we'll cover the ground rules of personal finance in a way that won't have you falling asleep over spreadsheets. The process is practical and straightforward, designed to give you a clear understanding of your financial situation and how to manage it effectively.

Crafting Your First Budget: A Step-by-Step Guide

Understanding Your Income

The first step to understanding your finances is knowing your income. Income includes everything from the money you make at a part-time gig, the cash grandma slips you on your birthday, to scholarships or stipends. Each source adds a layer to your financial foundation. Make a list of these sources because this breakdown is crucial for making informed decisions about allocating your resources effectively.

Tracking Your Expenses

We are now ready to look at your expenses. This isn't about frantically recording every cent you spend; it's about understanding spending categories. Divide your expenses into essentials (rent, groceries, utilities) and non-essentials (eating out, subscriptions, impulse buys). This categorization helps you see where you can make alterations to ensure that your income stretches through the month. You can spot trends by tracking your expenses. Maybe you're spending a small fortune on takeout, or those spontaneous online shopping sprees are tallying up. Recognizing these patterns is the first step toward managing them.

Setting Realistic Goals

Goal setting is your financial compass. Goals can range from short-term (saving for a concert ticket or new sneakers) to long-term (putting money away for college or a car). The key is to set realistic targets. If your budget shows you have $300 left each month after essentials, planning to save $400 is unrealistic and setting yourself up for disappointment. Aim for something achievable. Maybe start with saving $150 each month. Achievable goals keep morale high and financial stress low.

Adjusting and Adapting

Lastly, let's tackle the reality of financial flux. Your financial situation today might differ next year, next month, or even next week. Life throws curveballs—unexpected expenses like a car repair or changes in income like a new job. Adaptability in your budgeting is crucial. This means regularly revisiting and adjusting your budget to reflect your current financial reality. It's about being prepared. Adaptability allows you to confidently face these changes, knowing that your budget can accommodate them.

Reflection Section: Your Financial Snapshot

Take a moment now. Grab a pen and paper, or open a spreadsheet if you're technologically inclined. List all your income sources, and then track where you've spent money in the last month. Categorize these expenses. How does it feel seeing where your money is going? Surprising? Expected?

Use this snapshot to consider one realistic financial goal for the next month. Write it down, pin it up. It's your first step toward financial literacy and freedom.

In this chapter, we've begun laying the foundation for your financial stability with a straightforward approach to budgeting. As you move forward, remember that budgeting isn't about restricting freedom; it's about creating it. With every step, you're building confidence, not just in managing money but in managing your life and its challenges. With the basics in hand, you're well on your way to becoming financially aware and savvy.

Understanding Credit Scores and How to Build Yours

Every time you swipe your card, make an online purchase, or open an account, any non-cash financial transaction is recorded by algorithms that record your financial trustworthiness. Late account payments or defaulting on a debt detracts from your financial credibility. However, payments made on time and not running into your bank overdraft facility build on your financial trustworthiness. A credit score is a three-digit number that tells potential lenders everything they need to know about how good you are at handling your money. That score can open doors for borrowing opportunities and more.

So, what exactly is a credit score? Think of it as a financial report card with a result ranging from 300 to 850. The higher your score, the more financially trustworthy you are perceived to be. Why should you care? Because this little number affects your ability to do adult things like leasing a car, buying a home, or sometimes even landing that dream job. It can also influence how much interest you pay on loans and credit cards. A good credit score can save you a lot of money and hassle down the road, making it less of a financial pinch when you need to make big moves.

Let's discuss what feeds into this score. The most significant chunk—about 35%—is your payment history. This is a record of whether or not you've paid past credit accounts on time. Missed payments, bankruptcy, foreclosures … these financial missteps can seriously affect your score. Next up, weighing in at 30% is your credit utilization ratio. This is a fancy way of saying how much of your available credit you're using. Maxing out your credit cards can harm your score.

Building a good credit history takes time and careful planning. Start small. Consider applying for a secured credit card, where the credit limit is typically the deposit amount. It's a low-risk way to show you can handle credit wisely. Make small purchases and pay off the balance in full each month. This demonstrates responsibility and keeps your credit utilization low.

However, be wary of the common pitfalls. It's easy to fall into the trap of opening too many credit accounts at once. Each time you apply for a new line of credit, it can cause a small dip in your score. Do it too many times, and it starts to look like you're desperate for credit, which is a red flag for lenders. Also, avoid the temptation to only pay the minimum on your credit card. This approach can lead to ballooning balances and hefty interest charges. Remember, the goal is to use credit to build a credit history, not to buy items you don't need and can't afford.

Keeping your credit score healthy is crucial in solidifying your financial stability and ensuring you have the freedom to make choices that align with your ambitions and dreams.

Saving Strategies for Short-Term Goals: Tips and Tricks

When we talk about financial goals, it's like envisioning a personal treasure hunt, where X marks the spot for both short-term desires and long-term dreams. But let's zoom in on those short-term goals for now—those are the goals you'd like to hit in the near future. Maybe it's the latest smartphone, a concert ticket, or even a road trip with friends next summer. These aren't the hefty, life-altering ambitions like buying a house or retiring early, but they are immediate enough to keep you motivated.

Short-term goals

Understanding short-term goals is all about recognizing needs that will crop up sooner rather than later. They're typically things you're aiming to achieve within a year or so. Setting these goals gives you a clear target and helps prevent frivolous spending. Imagine you're saving for that new smartphone. Every time you're tempted to splurge on a fancy dinner out, you might think twice, considering how many more gigs of storage or extra camera features you could get if you just added that dinner money to your smartphone fund instead.

Compound interest

You might ask, what is compound interest? It's the interest you earn on your original money and the interest that money has already earned. Think of it as your money making its own money over time. For short-term goals, compound interest might not seem important because the timeline is shorter, but it can still give your savings a nice little boost. For instance, let's say you deposit $1,000 into a high-yield savings account with an interest rate of 2% compounded annually. At the end of the year, you have your initial $1,000 plus an extra $20 from interest. If you keep it there, the next year, you'll earn interest on $1,020, and so it grows.

High-yield savings accounts

A high-yield savings account is just one of the tools you can use to stash money for short-term goals. This type of account offers higher interest rates than regular savings accounts, meaning your money grows faster. You won't get rich off the interest, but it's a step up from the pennies traditional savings accounts offer.

Budgeting applications

Another great tool is budgeting apps. These apps can connect to your bank accounts, track your spending, and help you allocate funds to various goals. They visually display how close you are to reaching your savings targets, which can be a motivational boost. It's like having a progress bar on a game—it keeps you playing until you hit that next level, or in this case, your next financial goal.

***

Saving as a habit

Lastly, turning saving into a habit might be the real answer to financial health. It's about making saving as routine as brushing your teeth. An effective method is setting up an automatic transfer to your savings account right after you receive your paycheck. Think of it as paying your future self first. Even if it's a small amount, it adds up, and over time, it gets easier as you adjust to your slightly smaller spending pool. Another tip is to set daily, weekly, or monthly savings goals. These can be as simple as saving the $5 you might normally spend on a coffee every Friday. It might mean brewing at home and tossing those saved dollars into your travel fund. Little actions add up, and before you know it, you're not just dreaming about that road trip or fancy gadget—you're actively making it happen.

In summary, tackling short-term financial goals isn't just about putting money aside. It's about strategic moves like setting clear, achievable objectives, making the most of interest through the right financial tools, and turning saving into a regular part of your life. This approach doesn't just lead to meeting goals; it builds a foundation of financial discipline that will benefit you immensely as life rolls out more complex challenges and bigger dreams to chase.

Basic Investing for Beginners: Where to Start

So what does investing mean for you, the young adult? Investing isn't just for the suit-and-tie crowd; it's for anyone with a couple of bucks and a dream of building wealth, including you.

Investment fundamentals are the building blocks of making your money work for you. Stocks, bonds, and mutual funds might sound like a foreign language now, but they are actually pretty straightforward once you break them down. Stocks are essentially small parts of a company. When you buy stock, you're buying a little slice of that company, which, fingers crossed, will grow in value over time. On the other hand, bonds are like giving a loan to a company or government, and they pay you back with interest. Mutual funds are the party platters of the investment world—they mix a variety of stocks and bonds into one package, managed by someone who hopefully knows what they're doing.

Risks and rewards

It is crucial that we chat about risk versus reward—the tightrope of investing. Generally, the higher the potential return, the higher the risk. Stocks can swing high and low, offering the thrill of significant gains but also the potential for losses. Bonds are more of a slow and steady wins-the-race kind of deal; they are generally safer but with smaller returns. Deciding where to put your money depends a lot on your risk tolerance. Are you the financial equivalent of a skydiver, or does a quiet afternoon reading in the park sound more your speed? Understanding this about yourself is crucial in shaping your investment strategy.

* * *

Choosing the right option for you

Let's keep it simple for those of you who are about to dip your toes into the investment pool. Index funds are a great starting point. These funds mimic the performance of a specific index, like the S&P 500, so instead of betting on one company, you're spreading your risk across the market. Another user-friendly option is automated investment apps, often called robo-advisors. These apps use algorithms to manage your investments based on your risk tolerance and goals. It's like having a financial advisor in your pocket, minus the hefty fees.

But where do you start your investment education journey? The Internet is awash with resources, but tread carefully—reliable information is key. Websites like Investopedia offer clear explanations on just about every financial topic under the sun. For a deeper dive, books such as "The Intelligent Investor" by Benjamin Graham provide timeless advice on investing wisely. Suppose you're more of a visual learner. In that case, YouTube channels such as 'The Plain Bagel' can break down complex topics into digestible videos. And, of course, there are courses—many community colleges and online platforms like Coursera offer classes on investing basics that can provide a structured learning path.

Investing might seem daunting at first, but with a little knowledge and the right tools, it can become as routine as checking your social media feeds. Remember, the goal here isn't just to stash your cash but to make it grow. Whether you're saving up for a big trip, a new car, or a financially secure future, understanding investing is a crucial step.

Smart Spending: How to Evaluate Needs vs. Wants

Figuring out everything about financial responsibility might feel a bit like playing a game of "real life" Monopoly. You start with some cash, make decisions along the way—some good, some bad—and hope you don't end up broke by the time you pass "Go." One of the trickiest parts is separating your needs from your wants. We've all been there, standing in a store or browsing online, wrestling with the decision of whether to buy that trendy gadget or shiny pair of shoes. It feels like the ultimate showdown between the angel of necessity on one shoulder and the devil of splurge on the other.

So, how do we differentiate between needs and wants? It's simpler than you might think. Needs are your non-negotiables—rent, food, basic clothing, transportation costs, and essential utilities. Wants, on the other hand, are all the extras. They're the Netflix subscription, the weekend getaways, the latest iPhone, or that overpriced coffee you swear tastes better when someone else makes it. Recognizing this distinction is the first step toward smart spending. It's about acknowledging that while wants can bring short-term happiness, needs must come first to ensure long-term stability.

We are now ready to talk about mindful spending practices. Have you ever heard of the 30-day rule? It's a gem for making sure you're not caught in the impulse-buying trap. Here's how it works: when you feel the urge to buy something that's not a necessity, you pause. Jot it down on a list or put it in your online cart—and then you wait for 30 days. If, after a month, that burning desire for the item is still there and it fits into your budget consider getting it. You'll often find that the impulse fades, and you save yourself some cash for items you truly need or for savings. This practice isn't about delaying gratification; it's about refining it.

Allocating funds for discretionary spending without sabotaging your financial goals is like giving yourself a well-deserved treat without overindulging. It's possible, with a bit of foresight. Each month, once your needs are covered and you've set aside a portion for savings, what remains can be your discretionary fund. This is your playground. The key here is balance. If you overspend one month, adjust accordingly the next. It's not about cutting out fun; it's about enjoying it responsibly so you don't end up with regrets.

Impulse buying can be a tough habit to kick. Try setting waiting periods for different spending tiers. For instance, for purchases under $50, wait one day; for those up to $100, wait three days; for more expensive indulgences, wait a week or more. During this time, evaluate if the item is a want or a need, consider your current financial state, and check if it aligns with your financial goals. Additionally, keeping a wish list can be incredibly effective. It allows you to jot down things you desire and periodically review this list to see if you still want them or if they were just fleeting desires. This method not only curbs impulse spending but also prioritizes your wants so that you spend on what truly matters to you in the long run.

Understanding and practicing these strategies transforms how you handle money, turning you from a spontaneous spender into a savvy saver. It empowers you to make decisions that align with your financial goals, ensuring that your bank account remains as healthy as your spending habits. With a clear understanding of needs versus wants, a 30-day rule on hand, and strategic budgeting for fun, you're well-equipped to navigate the consumer world. As you get better at distinguishing between whims and necessities, you'll find that managing money isn't just about saving—it's about spending wisely, where each dollar spent brings you a step closer to both financial stability and genuine happiness.

Navigating Student Loans: Payment Plans and Forgiveness Programs

Diving into the world of student loans can be daunting, and it sometimes feels like you will never be debt-free. Student loans, while often necessary, come with their own set of rules that you need to understand.

In America, there are two main types of loans: federal and private. Federal loans have fixed interest rates and come with several borrower protections, such as income-driven repayment plans and possibilities for deferment. These loans are typically your best bet because of their flexibility and lower interest rates. Private loans, typically offered by banks, credit unions, and other financial institutions, are often offered with variable interest rates and fewer protections, which can be risky. Both types have their place in your financial strategy, but knowing which type to opt for at which time is important.

We need to discuss repayment plans sooner or later because you'll need to pay the lender for whatever type of loan you choose. Federal loans offer several repayment options, each with its own set of moves. The Standard Repayment Plan, for instance, can be paid off in 10 years with fixed payments. If that pace feels too brisk, income-driven repayment plans adjust your monthly payments based on your income and family size—these can extend to 20 or 25 years. However, private loans typically don't offer such flexibility, and you'll need to check with your lender about repayment options.

Loan Forgiveness and Assistance Programs

For federal loans, programs such as Public Service Loan Forgiveness (PSLF) can erase your remaining debt after you make 120 qualifying payments while working full-time for a qualifying employer (think government organizations and non-profits). Forgiveness programs are also for teachers and those in other public service careers. Remember, these programs have rules, so you'll need to find out if you qualify.

Default

Defaulting on your student loans can haunt you for years. To ensure that doesn't happen, consider setting up automatic payments, which can sometimes even qualify you for a lower interest rate. If you hit a rough patch, don't hesitate to contact your lawyer about deferment or forbearance options. It's better to take a breather than to cease payment.

Navigating the world of student loans is no small feat. It requires patience, persistence, and a good understanding of your options. Whether you're dealing with federal or private loans, knowing how to manage them can lead to a more controlled financial future. Remember, every financial institution has a unique set of rules, so find the repayment plan and forgiveness opportunities that best suit your ability to achieve your financial goals. With the right moves, you can turn what seems like an overwhelming burden into a manageable debt, keeping your financial health intact.

Notes

2
Achieving Financial Independence

"The goal isn't more money. The goal is living life on your terms."

— Chris Brogan

Ah, financial independence, the holy grail of adulting. It's that sweet spot where your money starts working for you, rather than you hustling non-stop for every dime. But some groundwork must be laid before you can sip cocktails on a beach while your investments multiply. It starts with what you know best—your passions and interests. Your love for graphic design, coding, baking, or even your knack for tutoring can be more than just hobbies; they can be your ticket to financial freedom. Let's explore how you can turn these passions into profits.

Side Hustles: Turning Passions into Profits

Coming up with a viable idea

Imagine turning your love for handmade crafts into a buzzing Etsy store or your weekend baking marathons into a profitable pop-up café. Sounds thrilling, doesn't it? But before diving headfirst into the entrepreneurial pool, it's crucial to explore your interests. This is about connecting the dots between what you enjoy and what can generate income. Start by listing activities that energize you—those you can spend hours on without looking at the clock. Now, think about which of these have market demand. Love playing video games? Consider streaming or coaching. Adore fashion? How about starting a vintage clothing resell business? The key is to align your skills with interests that people are willing to pay for.

Setting realistic expectations

Now that you've pinpointed your potential hustle, it's time to set up shop. But don't just launch a website or start printing business cards before laying a solid foundation. The first step is to create a budget. Calculate start-up costs, from materials to marketing, and figure out how much you'll need to keep the business running until you start to realize a profit. Speaking of profit, pricing your products or services correctly is crucial. Research what others in the market charge and position yourself competitively. Remember, while undercutting might attract initial customers, you're here to make a profit, not just break even. Setting these realistic expectations will keep you prepared and grounded in your journey.

Marketing

In today's digital age, social media is your best friend. Use platforms that align with your business, such as Instagram for visual ventures like photography and LinkedIn for professional services such as consulting. Engage with your potential customers, use relevant hashtags, and, most importantly, be consistent. Your brand is your promise to your customer; make it memorable and trustworthy.

Work-Life Balance

A side hustle isn't your whole life; it's part of it. Manage your time by setting specific hours for your side business. Use tools like Google Calendar or Trello to block out time for work and play if you find yourself constantly working without time off. It's tempting to let the hustle consume you, especially when it starts paying off, but remember, burnout is real. Keep your social life, studies, and side hustle in a harmonious balance, and you're more likely to achieve success in all areas. This balance will keep you reassured and in control of your journey.

Legal and Financial Considerations

Let's talk legality and taxes before you get too deep into the hustle groove. Ignoring these issues can cripple your business. Depending on your hustle, you might need a business license or permit, and if you are employed, ensure that your employer is okay with you having a small private business. It is unlikely that you will be able to run your enterprise at your place of work. Check with your local authorities about what's required. As for taxes, they can be a labyrinth, but navigating them correctly means you won't get a nasty surprise from the IRS. Consider using accounting software or hiring a professional if your budget allows. Keep records of every transaction, no matter how small. When tax season rolls around, you'll be ready.

Launching and managing a side hustle is like planting a garden. It starts with a seed—the idea, nourished by hard work and resilience, eventually blossoming into something that sustains you and brings joy and fulfillment. It's about leveraging what you already love doing, adding a sprinkle of business savvy, and watching as your financial independence takes root. With each step, you're not just earning extra dollars but building a life where work and passion fruitfully coexist.

Negotiating Your First Salary: Do's and Don'ts

Research The position you are applying for to know the going rate for your role in your geographic area. Start by visiting websites such as Glassdoor, PayScale, or LinkedIn Salaries, where you can input your job title, experience level, and location to see what others in your field are earning. This isn't just about numbers; it's about understanding your worth in the marketplace. This knowledge empowers you to confidently state your salary expectations, not as a whim, but as an informed professional stance.

Now, on to the art of negotiation. This is where finesse meets figures. When you're discussing numbers, be direct and assertive. This isn't the time for shy glances or mumbled words. Use phrases like, "Based on my research and experience, my expectation for a salary is in the range of X to

Y." Remember, the first number you say aloud is often considered the anchor of the negotiation, so aim a little higher within reason. You're providing a starting point, but leave room to maneuver. And here's a cheeky insider tip: try not to round off the figures. Saying you expect a salary of $47,750 rather than $48,000 might sound oddly specific, but it gives the impression that you've calculated your worth down to the last penny, which can be surprisingly persuasive.

Benefits and/or perquisites

Understanding benefits and compensation beyond the paycheck is your next strategic move. Benefits such as health insurance, retirement plans, bonuses, and even flexible working conditions can be goldmines. For instance, a robust health plan might save you more money in the long run than a slight bump in salary. The offer may include opportunities for professional development, stock options, or enhanced parental leave, which are particularly valuable. When evaluating the offer, consider the total value of the package, which includes not just the salary but also the value of these benefits. Ask yourself how these benefits align with your long-term personal and career goals. This holistic view makes a seemingly lower salary offer much more attractive.

Knowing your worth

What if the negotiation turns sour? Knowing when to walk away from a job offer is as crucial as learning how to clinch one. This might seem counterintuitive, especially if you've been job hunting for a while. However, clinging to a role that undervalues your skills or doesn't meet your essential financial needs can cause dissatisfaction and stress. Watch out for red flags like inflexibility on salary despite valid arguments, vague promises of future raises without concrete commitment, or a benefits package that needs key elements like health insurance. These signs might indicate that it's time to politely decline and continue your search. After all, the right job isn't just about filling your wallet; it's about fitting your life. However, you must be realistic and objective about your value to a company. As a newcomer, you cannot view yourself as being on par with an experienced employee in that field. Graduating at the top of your class does not mean you can enter a job and function like a seasoned employee. Book learning does not necessarily equip you for the practical side of things.

Navigating salary negotiations is a crucial skill, not just for your first job but throughout your career. It requires a mixture of planning, preparation, confidence, and tact. By doing your homework, presenting your case clearly, understanding the full compensation package, and recognizing when to walk away, you're not just bargaining for a few extra dollars. You're setting the stage for your financial future and ensuring your career path is rewarding and respectful. So, take a deep breath, muster your confidence, and step into that negotiation room, ready to make your case. With the proper preparation and mindset, you're not just securing a salary; you're investing in your worth.

Essential Insurance Policies for Young Adults

When navigating the maze of adult responsibilities, you'll quickly find that insurance serves as protection when things go sideways, and understanding what types of insurance you need is essential to avoiding financial disaster.

Let's start with health insurance. Health is unpredictable, no matter how invincible you feel doing your morning yoga or bench pressing at the gym. One unexpected medical emergency can set you back thousands if you're not covered. Health insurance can come through an employer, a parent's plan (until you turn 26), or the marketplace established by the Affordable Care Act. It's like having a safety net that catches you if you suddenly find yourself needing a bunch of medical tests or, heaven forbid, a prolonged stay in hospital.

The next type of interest is auto insurance. If you have a car, chances are it means more to you than any other possession because it represents your freedom to come and go as you please. Vehicle insurance protects you against financial loss if you're involved in an accident. It's not just about fixing dings and dents from that pole you didn't see; it's about protecting yourself from the potentially colossal costs of damaging other vehicles, property, or, worse, injuring someone. Most states require you to have at least basic auto insurance, so this isn't just a good-to-have; it's a must-have.

Moving on to renters' insurance. If you're renting your home, this is the shield for your belongings. Your landlord's insurance likely covers the building you live in but not what's inside your living space. Renters' insurance covers the loss of your possessions in the case of theft, fire, or other disasters. Think about it: could you afford to replace your laptop, bike, or other valuables if they were destroyed? For the cost of a couple of movie tickets a month, renters' insurance gives you the peace of mind that you will be able to replace your possessions in the case of a disaster.

Now that you know the types of insurance that should be on your radar, how do you figure out what you really need? Consider your lifestyle and financial situation. If you're a digital nomad with a laptop as your primary asset, renters' insurance is a good idea. Drive a car daily? Don't skimp on auto insurance. Regularly scaling cliffs or doing backflips on a BMX? Health insurance is a no-brainer. Assessing your needs isn't about fearing the worst; it's about preparing to keep your life on track even when unexpected events try to derail it.

Comparing insurance policies can feel as daunting as choosing a new cell phone plan—there are so many options that it's tempting to pick one and hope for the best. Resist this urge. Start by comparing what the different policies cover. Look at the limits and deductibles. A low premium might seem appealing until you realize it comes with a high deductible, which could end up costing you more in the event of a claim. Use comparison websites or talk to an insurance broker who can explain the fine print, such as what's actually covered under "accidental damage" or how different riders and add-ons can enhance your coverage. You want the best combination of options to avoid future disasters.

Lastly, remember that insurance is a crucial financial tool. It's about shifting the risk of financial loss from you to the insurance company. In exchange for a relatively small payment, you're buying peace of mind and protection from potentially catastrophic costs that could throw your financial goals off track. Whether it's a fender bender, a stolen laptop, or a physical injury, having the right insurance policies means you can focus on recovery without the added stress of financial ruin.

Navigating the world of insurance is part of building your financial resilience. While it might not be the most exhilarating adulting task, understanding and investing in the right insurance coverage ensures that when life inevitably throws curveballs, you're not just ready—you're financially armored. Take the time to assess, compare, and choose wisely.

Planning for Retirement in Your 20s: A Beginner's Guide

Retirement might seem like something so far in the future that you don't have to think about it for many years. However, planning for retirement in your 20s isn't about sucking the fun out of your youth; it's about making sure that when you can no longer work, you don't have to worry about how you'll pay rent or find another job to make ends meet.

So, why start now? Compound interest is that wonderful phenomenon that makes your money grow exponentially over time. Your retirement savings works in a similar manner as planting a tree, nourishing it, and seeing it grow and carry fruit. The money you invest now has decades to increase in value, thanks to interest building upon interest. If you start saving just a little bit now, you could end up with a lot more than if you start saving more money later. It's like turning a tiny acorn into a mighty oak, but in this case, the acorn is your cash, and the oak is your financial freedom down the line.

There are several types of retirement accounts, and picking the right one can make a big difference. You've probably heard of 401(k)s and IRAs, right? These are the big players in the retirement game. A 401(k) is often offered through your employer, who might even match a part of your contributions, and it allows you to save directly from your paycheck, pre-tax. That means you can lower your taxable income while saving for the future—a double win. Then there's the Individual Retirement Account (IRA), which you can set up yourself. You've got choices here, too: a Traditional IRA, where you contribute pre-tax dollars just like a 401(k), or a Roth IRA, where you put in money after taxes but then never pay taxes on those funds again, even when you withdraw them in retirement. Deciding between these can depend on your current income and how you expect it to change over time. Lower income now and hoping to be in a higher tax bracket later? Roth might be your best bet. Higher income now and expecting a drop later? Traditional could be what you need. Speak to someone who knows their way around the different options and can help you choose the best option.

The next question is how much you should actually be saving. While the exact number can vary depending on your lifestyle, income, and when you want to retire, a good rule of thumb is to save at least 15% of your pre-tax income each year. It sounds like a chunk, and it is, but remember, that includes any employer match in your 401(k), which can help you hit that target faster. The key is consistency—make it a habit and set up automatic transfers to your retirement account each month. Most of the time, these accounts will not allow you to withdraw money until retirement age.

Let's talk investment options within these accounts because letting your savings sit there without growing is like planting that tree in the shade—it won't thrive. Most retirement accounts offer a range of investment options, from more aggressive stocks to safer bonds. When you're young, you can generally afford to be a bit more daring about where you put your money because you have time to ride out the market's ups and downs. Think about it: stocks might be more volatile, but they also offer the potential for higher returns. This can significantly boost your retirement fund over decades. As you get closer to retirement age, you can start shifting your investments to more conservative options, protecting what you've accumulated from significant market swings.

Investing in your retirement is investing in your future freedom. It's about making choices today that will empower your older self to have financial security and make the most of life after work. Whether it's traveling the world, indulging in hobbies, or simply enjoying the peace of mind that comes with financial stability, starting early gives you the best shot at a golden retirement.

The Art of Frugal Living Without Sacrificing Joy

Frugality is about becoming a clever spender and a connoisseur of cost-cutting without sacrificing joy. It's about not wasting money but rather making value-driven choices that bring you joy while still maintaining a healthy bank balance.

Frugality, in its essence, is not about choosing the cheapest option; instead, it's about prioritizing your spending in a way that aligns with your most cherished values and goals. It's choosing to cook a gourmet meal at home with friends instead of dining out. It involves selecting experiences and purchases for their immediate appeal and lasting impact on your happiness and financial well-being. This approach transforms frugality from a mere exercise in spending less to a more fulfilling practice of spending smart.

However, there's a thin line between being frugal and being cheap, and avoiding crossing is crucial. Being cheap is about spending the least amount possible, often at the expense of quality, ethics, or long-term benefits. For instance, buying a poorly made pair of shoes that will fall apart in a month is cheap. Investing in a quality pair that lasts for years is frugal. The frugal choice often requires an upfront investment, but it pays dividends in durability, satisfaction, and, over time, cost savings. It's about knowing that spending a little more now can actually save you money down the road.

Embracing a frugal lifestyle doesn't mean giving up what you love; instead, it means tweaking your habits to enhance your financial and personal well-being. Consider the daily coffee run. Buying a $5 coffee every weekday adds up to about $100 a month. Now, what if you purchased a quality coffee maker and brewed it yourself? You'd not only save money but also have the opportunity to become a skilled barista in your own right. And what about entertainment? Instead of hitting the movie theater every week, why not host a movie night at home with friends? You'll still enjoy the latest films but with the added joy of good company and home-cooked snacks.

Frugal living isn't about denial; it's about redefining what you truly value and aligning your spending accordingly. It's about finding creative, fulfilling ways to enjoy life while keeping your financial goals on track. This mindset shift from "cutting costs" to "optimizing spending" can make all the difference, turning what could feel like sacrifice into a rewarding challenge.

Resources for Frugal Living

Navigating a frugal lifestyle can be much more fun and effective with a community or some guiding resources. Countless books, blogs, and communities turn frugality into an art form. Consider picking up a copy of "The Millionaire Next Door" by Thomas J. Stanley and William D. Danko. It's a classic that dives deep into the habits of people who've successfully amassed wealth through wise living, not high earning. Blogs like "Mr. Money Mustache" offer a cheeky take on frugal living while providing practical tips on how to cut expenses without cutting joy from your life.

Online communities, especially forums such as Reddit's r/Frugal, can also offer support, inspiration, and a treasure trove of frugality hacks. These platforms allow you to connect with like-minded individuals who share their experiences and advice on living well for less. Whether you're looking for the best budget recipes, DIY home repair tips, or the cheapest travel hacks, these communities can be invaluable.

Engaging with these resources can provide you with practical tips and a sense of belonging and motivation. Knowing you're not alone in your quest to live better for less is comforting and encouraging. By researching the expertise and experiences of others, you can refine your own approach to frugality, tailor it to your personal aspirations and lifestyle, and perhaps even share your journey to inspire others.

Incorporating frugal practices into your life is less about restricting yourself and more about enriching your lifestyle in a financially sustainable way. It's a proactive, creative, and deeply rewarding way to enhance your financial independence and personal satisfaction. By redefining frugality, distinguishing it from mere cheapness, and making thoughtful lifestyle adjustments, you can enjoy a life full of richness—both in experiences and in your bank account—without the burden of unnecessary expenses.

Financial Health Check-ups: Quarterly Review Best Practices

Quarterly reviews are your financial system checks. They allow you to catch potential problems early, adjust strategies to better meet your goals, and celebrate milestones that keep you motivated. Start by setting a specific date each quarter that you dedicate to reviewing your finances, mark it on your calendar, and treat it as important as a job interview or a college exam. During these check-ups, you focus on key financial metrics that clearly show where you stand. It's not just about glancing at your bank account balance; it's about diving deep into how well you are sticking to your budget, the progress of your savings goals, the reduction of any debts, and how effectively your investments are performing.

One of the first metrics to scrutinize is your savings progress. Are you on track with the financial goals you set at the beginning of the year? Whether it's saving for a new laptop or setting aside money for an emergency fund, assess if your current savings rate will get you to your goal in the timeframe you planned. If you need more time to catch up, consider what adjustments you can make. It could be cutting back on non-essentials or finding additional streams of income, like a side gig. On the flip side, if you're ahead of schedule, consider setting new, more ambitious goals or exploring investment options to grow your savings faster.

Next, evaluate your spending patterns. Analyze your spending habits to identify areas where you can save without compromising your quality of life. Perhaps you're spending a lot on eating out. Could you reduce it by preparing more meals at home? You may also find a recurring subscription that you no longer use. Cancel it and redirect that money towards your savings. This isn't about penny-pinching; it's about making smart choices that align your spending with your financial goals.

Debt reduction is another critical area to review. Look at how much debt you've paid off and how much you still owe. Are you making progress at the rate you anticipated? If not, consider adjusting your debt repayment plan. You may need to allocate more money towards your debts or explore refinancing to lower interest rates. Remember, the faster you can get out of debt, the more resources you have available for saving and investing.

Tools for Tracking Financial Health

You need the right tools to keep tabs on all these metrics. Luckily, in the digital age, numerous apps and software are designed to make financial tracking and analysis relatively simple. Apps like Mint or YNAB (You Need A Budget) can be particularly helpful. They track your spending and savings, offer insights into your financial habits, and send alerts when you're deviating from your budget. For investment tracking, consider using apps like Personal Capital or Betterment. They provide a clear view of your investment performance and offer personalized advice based on your financial data.

Investing in these tools and reviewing your financial health regularly can significantly impact your ability to meet and exceed your financial goals. It's about taking proactive steps to cultivate a healthy financial future, ensuring that with each passing quarter, you're aware of your financial status and making informed decisions to maintain or improve it.

As we wrap up this chapter on achieving financial independence, remember that each section, from understanding insurance to planning for retirement, is about building layers of security and confidence in your financial journey. By integrating these practices, especially the regular financial health check-ups, you're not just dreaming of financial independence but actively constructing it, one informed decision at a time.

Looking ahead, we'll delve into building emotional resilience—an essential skill that complements your financial savvy. This will ensure that you're equipped economically, mentally, and emotionally to handle whatever life throws your way.

Notes

3
Building Emotional Strength

"You don't have to control your thoughts. You just have to stop letting them control you."

— Dan Millman

"The greatest glory in living lies not in never falling, but in rising every time we fall."

— Nelson Mandela

Imagine navigating the bustling streets of a big city for the first time. There's the cacophony of honking cars, the neon blur of speeding advertisements, and crowds of people, each marching to the beat of their urgent errands. It can be overwhelming, right? Now, picture your emotional health in a similar urban sprawl. Just as city streets are laden with potential stressors—like that taxi that almost splashed you from head to toe—so too is your journey into adulthood strewn with challenges that can frazzle your nerves. This chapter is about mastering the map of your emotional cityscape, identifying the stress potholes, and navigating them with the finesse of a seasoned urbanite.

Identifying and Managing Stress Triggers

Awareness is Key

First things first: spotting the stress triggers. It's about tuning in to your emotional weather station. What makes the pressure rise? Is it looming deadlines, social gatherings, or perhaps financial worries? Or maybe it's the fear of failure, the pressure to perform, or the uncertainty of the future? Recognizing these triggers is like spotting a storm cloud on the horizon—you know it's time to open your emotional umbrella. Keep a stress diary for a week or two; jot down moments when you feel overwhelmed, anxious, or irritable. Look for patterns. Does your stress spike during late-night study sessions or after scrolling through social media? Identifying these patterns is your first step in crafting an effective stress management strategy.

* * *

Stress Management Techniques

Now, let's talk about tackling stress. Imagine you're a DJ at the mixing desk of your life, and stress management techniques are your soundboard. Each slider and knob is a tool to adjust the bass, treble, and volume of your daily stressors. Deep breathing exercises, for instance, can help dial down the anxiety volume. Try the 4-7-8 technique: breathe in for four seconds, hold for seven, and exhale for eight. It's like hitting the slow-mo button on life's chaos. To practice this technique, find a comfortable position, close your eyes, and take a deep breath in through your nose for a count of four. Hold your breath for a count of seven. Then, exhale slowly and completely through your mouth for a count of eight. Repeat this cycle four times. Time management skills, on the other hand, can keep the tempo of your day harmonious and prevent those last-minute scrambles that crank up the stress decibels. Tools like digital planners or apps like Todoist can help orchestrate your day-to-day tasks with harmonious precision, ensuring each part—study, work, leisure—plays in perfect harmony.

Creating a Stress-Relief Plan

Crafting a personalized stress-relief plan is about creating a set of strategies that resonate with your stress triggers and soothe your psyche. Start with simple daily or weekly rituals that act as your stress buffers. It could be a morning run, a nightly journaling session, or a weekly yoga class. These activities are your emotional recharges, your breathers. But also plan for unexpected stress. Have a toolkit ready—perhaps a playlist of calming music, a stash of herbal teas, or a list of friends you can call when the emotional noise gets too loud. This plan isn't static; it evolves and adapts as the need arises, providing you with the reassurance and flexibility you need in your quest for tranquility.

Seeking Support

Finally, let's underscore the importance of support. Having a support network is crucial, whether it's friends, family, or professionals such as counselors and therapists. They are your backup when stress becomes too much to handle alone. These are the folks whose perspectives, advice, or just an empathetic ear you regard highly. The people you trust to have your back and steer you in the right direction. Don't hesitate to reach out. Sometimes, just verbalizing your stress can diminish its intensity, turning what feels like unmanageable anxiety into a calm that allows you to think things through and find your way back to peace. Remember, you're not alone in this journey.

In this ever-spinning world of responsibilities and expectations, understanding how to manage stress is as crucial as any academic skill or professional expertise. It's about more than just surviving; it's about thriving. Everyone experiences stress. You just need to learn to manage it and what works for you. Mastering stress-reduction techniques, crafting a personalized stress-relief plan, and leaning on your support network can help you to cope and pave the way to serenity and success.

The Power of Mindfulness: Techniques for Relieving Anxiety

Ever felt like your mind is a browser with a hundred tabs open? Everything is loading, notifications are buzzing, and you can't find the mute button? That's anxiety in a nutshell. Imagine if you could slow it all down, maybe even enjoy one tab at a time. That's where mindfulness comes into play—a simple yet profound way of tuning into the present and bringing a sense of calm to your mind.

Understanding mindfulness begins with breaking down the essence of the practice. It's about being fully present, aware of where we are and what we're doing, and not overly reactive to what's going around us. Think of it as mental poise, allowing you to move through your day gracefully, even amidst stress. It's less about emptying your mind and more about focusing it—letting go of the noise to tune into what matters in the here and now. This mental shift doesn't just help reduce anxiety; it enhances overall well-being, making it easier to enjoy life and handle challenges.

Let's start with something as simple as breathing. Meditation, specifically mindfulness meditation, is like going to the gym for your mental health. It strengthens your mind's ability to concentrate and relax. Begin with just five minutes a day. Find a quiet spot, sit comfortably, close your eyes, and focus on your breath. Inhale deeply, feel your chest expand, and exhale slowly, feeling the air leave your lungs. Thoughts will intrude, but that's okay. The goal isn't to block them out entirely but to gently bring your focus back to your breathing whenever you notice your mind wandering. It's this act of refocusing that builds your mindfulness muscle.

Mindful walking is another great practice, especially if sitting still isn't your thing. It can turn a simple walk into a revitalizing ritual. Focus on the sensation of walking—the feel of the ground under your feet, the rhythm of your steps, the sounds around you. It's about really being in that walk, not just using it as a transition from point A to B. Each step is a way to ground yourself in the moment.

Incorporating Mindfulness into Daily Life

Bringing mindfulness into your daily life doesn't require changing your routine but rather your approach to routine activities. It could be as simple as turning off autopilot while brushing your teeth. Feel the bristles against your gums, taste the mint of the toothpaste, and listen to the sound of brushing. When you eat, really taste your food. Notice the textures, flavors, and temperature. Eating becomes more enjoyable when you're truly present with it rather than mechanically shoveling food in while binge-watching a series.

The impact of these mindfulness practices on anxiety is profound. They teach you to respond to stress rather than react to it. You begin to notice the signs of anxiety early—your heart racing, your breath quickening—and you have the tools to dial it back, to tell your body, "It's okay. We've got this." Over time, these practices can lower your baseline anxiety levels, making calm your default setting rather than something you have to strive for.

Reflecting on how mindfulness affects your anxiety and well-being is crucial. It's about recognizing the subtle shifts. Maybe you find yourself pausing to breathe when work gets hectic, or perhaps you're not as rattled by a change in plans as you used to be. These are signs that mindfulness is weaving its peace through your life. Keep a journal of these observations. Write about moments when mindfulness made a difference. This reinforces the value of your practice and encourages you to continue and deepen your mindfulness journey.

Mindfulness isn't a magic pill for anxiety. Still, with consistent practice, it offers a powerful way to manage stress and enhance one's quality of life. By integrating mindfulness into one's daily activities, one transforms ordinary moments into opportunities for peace and presence, building a life that is less stressed and more deeply enjoyed.

Overcoming Fear of Failure: Lessons in Resilience

Let's face it—the fear of failure can creep into your thoughts at the most inopportune moments. But what if I told you that this fear could actually be turned into a secret weapon? Redefining failure is not about denying its discomfort but about shifting perspective to see it as a necessary part of the learning and growing process. Think of failure as the challenge that propels you and encourages you to try harder.

The first step in this redefinition is to strip failure of its power to invoke fear. Consider it a valuable feedback mechanism instead of viewing it as a humiliating end. Whenever something doesn't go as planned, it's an opportunity to gather intel—what worked, what didn't, and what can be done differently next time. This approach transforms the fear of failure from a roadblock into a stepping stone, leading towards improvement and innovation. For instance, if you bombed a presentation, instead of spiraling into an "I'm just not good at this" mindset, analyze the situation. Maybe you were unprepared, or perhaps anxiety got the better of you. Each of these revelations guides what to focus on for next time.

Building resilience is akin to building muscle; it requires consistent effort and the proper techniques. One of the most effective strategies is setting realistic goals. While it's great to shoot for the stars, setting goals that are out of reach can set you up for a crash landing. Instead, set achievable goals to build your confidence. Attaining these goals creates a pattern of small successes, which reinforce the belief that you can handle challenges and achieve your aims. Maintaining a growth mindset is another crucial element in building resilience. This mindset revolves around the belief that abilities and intelligence can be developed through dedication and hard work. It's about embracing challenges, persisting in the face of setbacks, and viewing effort as a path to mastery. It's the difference between thinking, "I'm just not a math person," and "I can get better at math with practice and the right strategies."

Learn from your mistakes—this is where the real growth happens. It's easy to beat yourself up after a slip-up, but self-judgment only encourages discouragement. Instead, adopt a scientist's mindset. Observe and analyze your mistakes without emotional bias. What variables led to the error? Was it a lack of knowledge, a misjudgment of resources, or perhaps external factors you failed to consider? Understanding these can turn errors into valuable lessons, not just for avoiding future mistakes but for developing new strategies and approaches. For example, if you find procrastination is a recurring theme in your failures, dig deeper into why. Are you overwhelmed, disinterested, or perhaps afraid of the task at hand? Each insight provides a clue on how to adjust your approach for better outcomes in the future. At this stage, it is worth pointing out that you can't be an expert at everything. Recognize your strengths and weaknesses. Where you have a strength, someone else has a weakness, and working as a team can achieve goals you can't accomplish alone.

Finally, let's discuss celebrating progress and effort, not just outcomes. In a world that often highlights end results, it's easy to overlook the value of the journey. Celebrating the small victories and the effort you put in cultivates a sense of accomplishment and a positive mindset, regardless of the outcome. Did you make it halfway through a challenging book you previously would have given up on? That's a win. Despite feeling nervous, did you stand up and share an idea in a meeting? Another win. These moments deserve recognition because they symbolize your commitment to growth and resilience. They are the true indicators of your progress, showing who you are becoming, not just what you are achieving.

Embracing these practices reshapes your relationship with failure. It's no longer a shadow to be feared but a teacher to be heeded. By redefining failure, setting realistic goals, learning from mistakes, and celebrating effort, you build resilience that carries you through challenges and elevates your potential for success. With each step forward, you're crafting a narrative of growth, strength, and relentless perseverance, ready to face any twist the plot throws your way.

Developing a Positive Self-Image in the Social Media Age

In an era where your social media presence can feel as crucial as your real-life one, it's no exaggeration to say that the digital world can significantly sway your self-image and self-esteem. Imagine every like, comment, and follow as a mirror reflecting back at you—but not always the most accurate or kindest version of yourself. This constant barrage of digital feedback can skew our perceptions of ourselves, often more harshly than any real-life interaction would. It's like being in a funhouse of mirrors where every reflection is distorted by the filters and highlights reels of others' lives. The key here is recognizing that these platforms are designed to showcase the best, often unreal, moments. Comparing your behind-the-scenes to everyone else's highlight reel is like comparing your everyday life to a blockbuster movie; it's entertaining but not an accurate reflection of daily life.

Cultivating self-compassion in this hyper-connected world is akin to giving yourself a break—a real one, not just a five-minute pause between Instagram stories. It starts with talking to yourself like you would to a good friend. Notice when you're being self-critical, especially after scrolling through your feeds. Would you say those things to someone you care about? Probably not. So, why tell them to yourself? Practices such as journaling can be a powerful tool here. Try writing down the critical thoughts and challenging them. For example, if you think, "I'm not as interesting as people online," counter that by listing moments when you've been appreciated for your wit or kindness in real life. These exercises aren't about inflating your ego but correcting the imbalance social media often creates in how we see ourselves.

Developing healthy social media habits is crucial, not just for your time management but for your mental health. Start by auditing your social media usage. How much time are you really spending online? And more importantly, how does it make you feel? Apps that track your usage can be eye-opening. If you find that the hours are high and the mood is low post-scrolling, it's a sign to cut back. But it's not just about reducing screen time; it's about curating your consumption. Unfollow accounts that trigger insecurity or anxiety. Instead, fill your feed with content that uplifts and inspires. Follow accounts that focus on hobbies you love or offer positive affirmations. It's about turning your feed into a space that supports your well-being, not undermines it.

Seeking authentic connections, both online and offline, is about quality over quantity. It's easy to get caught up in the numbers game—counting friends, followers, likes. But meaningful connections are not a numbers game. They are about interactions that add value and warmth to your life. Online, seek out groups that share your interests, whether it's a love for books, a passion for sustainability, or a penchant for old movies. Engage genuinely. Offline, prioritize relationships that make you feel seen and supported. It could be a weekly coffee date with a friend or a family game night. These interactions are the antidote to the sometimes superficial connections of social media, providing depth, perspective, and a great deal of joy.

Navigating the complex web of self-image in the age of social media is no small feat. Still, with thoughtful strategies and intentional habits, it's not only possible but also incredibly rewarding. You build a resilient, positive self-image by fostering self-compassion, curating a healthier digital diet, and investing in genuine connections. In this ever-connected world, remember, the most important connection is the one you have with yourself.

Navigating Grief and Loss as a Young Adult

Grief is like an uninvited guest who shows up at the worst possible time, overstays, and doesn't abide by any of the usual social cues, such as that it's time to leave. Understanding grief is crucial because it's not just about feeling sad; it's a complex process that involves a kaleidoscope of emotions that can turn your world inside out. From denial, anger, bargaining, and depression to acceptance—these stages don't line up neatly and can't be checked off like tasks on a to-do list. They overlap, repeat, and sometimes, you might feel several at once. It's like being in the middle of a whirlwind, where moments of calm are punctuated by stormy bursts of emotion. Acknowledging that this is a natural response to loss is the first step toward managing this tumultuous experience. Grief is not a problem to be fixed; it's a process to be experienced, and understanding this can help you give yourself the grace to feel without judgment.

Self-care during grief is like crafting a personal lifeboat amid a storm. It's about finding what keeps you afloat in turbulent times. Start by recognizing that your energy levels and emotional bandwidth are likely not at their peak. Focus on the basics: eating nutritious meals, getting enough sleep, and some form of physical activity, even if it's just short walks. In the face of loss, these might seem trivial, but maintaining your physical well-being significantly supports your emotional resilience.

Find solace in routines; they can be comforting when everything feels chaotic. Perhaps maintaining a morning or bedtime routine can provide small anchors of normalcy. Additionally, creative expression can be incredibly therapeutic. Whether journaling, painting or even gardening, these activities offer a means to process complex feelings tangibly, helping to navigate your grief.

You need support during these times. Support groups connect you with others navigating similar grief in person or online. They provide a space to share your feelings and experiences, reducing the isolation often accompanying loss. Therapy can also help guide you through your grief. A therapist can offer professional insights and coping strategies tailored to your personal experience. Remember, seeking help is not a sign of weakness; it's a strategy for strength. It's about equipping yourself with the right tools and support to manage your grief effectively. And pay attention to the power of open conversations with loved ones. Sometimes, just verbalizing your feelings can lighten the emotional load. These conversations can also help others understand what you're going through and how they can support you.

Honoring loss is about creating a bridge between the past and the present, a way to keep the memory of loved ones alive while continuing to manage your daily routines. This can be as personal as setting up a small memorial with photos and mementos or as public as participating in a charity run in their memory. Maybe it's planting a tree or starting a scholarship fund—actions that commemorate those you've lost and create a legacy of love and resilience. It's important to remember them, not just in moments of sadness but also in acts of joy and celebration. This honoring is not about dwelling in the past but acknowledging that those we love continue to influence our lives, inspiring actions that weave their memories into the fabric of our daily existence.

Navigating grief and loss at any time in one's life, particularly as a young adult, is undeniably challenging. It tests your emotional depths and resilience in ways few other experiences can. But with the proper understanding, self-care strategies, support, and ways to honor your loss, you can navigate this complex journey with strength and grace. While the pain of loss may never entirely disappear, these strategies provide tools to manage grief in a way that honors your emotions and the memory of those lost, fostering healing and growth in the process.

Cultivating Joy: Practical Steps to Increase Happiness

Let's shift gears and talk about cultivating joy—something light yet profoundly impactful that brings happiness to your everyday life, regardless of the circumstances. It's about embracing the small, delightful parts of your day that, when strung together, create a feeling of overall contentment and happiness. It begins with identifying the sources of your joy, integrating gratitude, engaging actively with your community, and mastering the art of savoring life's beautiful moments.

Have you ever noticed how certain activities or people light you up from the inside? It could be that morning jog, strumming the guitar, or cooking a new recipe. Or it's the deep conversations with a close friend, or the belly laughs with your siblings. These are your personal joy triggers. You need to become more conscious of these activities and people and purposefully integrate more of them into your routine. Start by listing all the things and people that bring you joy. Be exhaustive. Next, look at your weekly schedule. Where can you carve out time for these joy-generating activities? Maybe it's waking up earlier to read, turning off your phone for an hour to connect with friends, or dedicating Sunday afternoons to a hobby. The aim is to make these activities routine.

Gratitude practice is about changing the lens through which you view your life, from what's missing to what's present. It's a powerful tool for shifting focus from the negatives to the positives, enhancing overall happiness. Start simple. Every night, make a note of the things you were grateful for that day;

there has to be something. They could be as profound as a supportive friend or as simple as a delicious lunch. Over time, this practice increases your awareness of life's blessings and conditions so that you can be more present and find joy even on tough days. You need to consciously appreciate the little things in life until it becomes second nature.

Engaging with Community

Joy often multiplies when shared. Engaging with your community, whether it's your neighborhood, school, an online community of like-minded individuals, or your family, can significantly amplify your sense of happiness. Participate in community activities—be it a local clean-up, a charity run, a neighborhood potluck, or a family get-together. Such activities foster a sense of belonging and purpose and connect you to others, creating a shared space for joy. Additionally, contributing to the community can provide a deep sense of satisfaction and pride, knowing that you are making a tangible difference in others' lives. It's a feedback loop where giving sparks joy, which inspires more giving, creating a spiral of positivity.

Mindful Enjoyment

Finally, the art of savoring—the mindful appreciation of experiences—can profoundly enhance your joy. Savoring is about fully engaging in the moment, whether you're watching a sunset, enjoying a meal, or listening to music. It's about noticing the details, the colors, the flavors, the sounds, and the emotions they evoke and allowing yourself to be fully immersed and affected by the experience. To practice, choose one daily routine activity and commit to experiencing it fully.

Turn off distractions and focus all your senses on the activity. Reflect on how it feels, what it reminds you of, and why it's enjoyable. This practice enhances joy in the moment and can also help create lasting memories that offer joy upon recollection.

Every small step in cultivating joy has a ripple effect, enhancing your happiness and overall well-being and often spilling over to the people around you. By identifying what brings you joy, practicing gratitude, engaging with your community, and savoring life's moments, you set the stage for a richer, more fulfilling life experience. These practices weave a safety net of positivity that holds you steady, even through life's inevitable ups and downs.

As this chapter closes, remember that the journey to increased happiness isn't about overhauling your entire life but about adding layers of joy through everyday choices and practices. These steps create a robust framework for a joyful existence, empowering you to navigate life with a light heart and an open mind. As we transition into the next chapter, keep the momentum of positivity going. Let's explore how these frameworks of joy can enhance personal and professional aspects of life, leading to a well-rounded, deeply satisfying life journey.

Notes

4
Fostering Healthy Relationships

"The most important thing in communication is hearing what isn't said."

— Peter Drucker

Imagine stepping into a vast space filled with people—each one unique. They all have likes and dislikes, strengths and weaknesses, joys and fears. Navigating this group of individuals requires the subtle art of communication. Making yourself heard is not about talking louder than anyone else; it's about ensuring that your words are impactful and meaningful, making connections as you move among them. Speak your truth, but listen carefully when others speak theirs. Effective communication, verbal and non-verbal, cultivate resilient and rewarding relationships. Remember, you have the power to shape these relationships to ensure they thrive.

Effective Communication: Beyond Words

Listening Skills

Let's start with the cornerstone of all great conversations—listening. Active listening, to be exact. Active listening is an all-in engagement: you listen with your ears, eyes, and heart. It's about hearing the words, noticing the tone, reading the body language, and understanding the emotions behind the words. This type of listening is like a superpower in any relationship because it makes the speaker feel valued and understood, paving the way for trust and openness. Follow the steps below to become an active listener.

- Focus entirely on the speaker.
- Avoid interrupting or planning your response while they're talking.
- Give feedback that shows you're engaged, like nodding your head or summarizing what you've heard to ensure you've got it right.
- Use the person's name when you respond to them.

This way, conversations transform from parallel monologues into dynamic communication. It's a fascinating process.

* * *

Expressing Needs Clearly

Now, let's move on to expressing your own needs and desires. This is where many of us stumble. You need to be clear and honest. But first, you need to understand your needs. Take a moment to reflect: What is it that you really want or need from your relationships? Once you've got a handle on this, craft your message in a direct yet considerate way. Use "I" statements to speak from your perspective without blaming or criticizing the other person. 'I' statements are a way of expressing your feelings and needs without making the other person feel attacked. For example, saying, "I feel upset when plans are canceled at the last minute," is more straightforward and less confrontational than "You're always flaking on plans!" This approach minimizes defensiveness and increases the chances of your needs being understood and met.

Nonverbal Communication

Words are undoubtedly powerful, but the silent signals we send can often speak louder than our loudest words. Nonverbal communication—your body language, facial expressions, and even your silence—plays a significant role in how your message is received. For instance, crossed arms might signal defensiveness, while maintaining eye contact shows confidence and interest. Other examples of nonverbal cues include nodding to show agreement, leaning forward to show interest, or fidgeting to show discomfort. Being mindful of your nonverbal cues and interpreting others' can significantly enhance your communicative effectiveness. Always be on the lookout for clues to how the other person is really feeling, as this facilitates more sensitive interactions.

Feedback and Constructive Criticism

Lastly, let's tackle the delicate art of feedback. Whether giving or receiving, feedback is essential for growth and improvement in any relationship. When giving feedback, focus on being constructive rather than critical. Highlight specific behaviors instead of making personal attacks. Frame your feedback with positives, suggest solutions, and be open to discussion. For example, instead of saying, "Your reports are always so sloppy," try, "I've noticed some errors in your reports. Perhaps reviewing them once more before submission could help?" When receiving feedback, remember that it's not an attack but an opportunity to learn and evolve. Listen openly, ask clarifying questions if necessary, and express gratitude for the chance to improve. This two-way street of constructive feedback can turn potential conflicts into powerful catalysts for personal and collective growth, fostering an optimistic and open mindset toward learning and improvement.

Navigating the complex world of relationships through effective communication is about more than just exchanging information; it's about connecting on a deeper level, understanding, and being understood. As you cultivate these skills, your interactions with others will flourish with trust, respect, and mutual growth.

Setting Boundaries: The Foundation for Healthy Relationships

Understanding what boundaries are is the first step in becoming secure within your personal space. Boundaries are the lines you draw around yourself to indicate what are acceptable behaviors, responses, and treatments from others. They help you protect your emotional energy, maintain self-respect, and foster healthy relationships. However, those around you also have such boundaries, and theirs might not be identical to yours. As much as you don't want them stepping over your boundaries, they don't want you to ignore theirs. You have to remain aware of what other people deem suitable behavior from you. This awareness and respect for others' boundaries is a key aspect of considerate and empathetic behavior in relationships.

Identifying your personal boundaries requires self-reflection and honesty. Start by considering your values and what makes you feel comfortable and safe. These are clues to where your boundaries should lie. For example, if honesty is a core value, a boundary might involve distancing yourself from those who consistently deceive or mislead you. Recognizing these needs isn't selfish; it's a form of self-care that preserves your well-being and respects your values.

Communicating these boundaries clearly and effectively to others can often feel daunting. It's like setting out your 'Do Not Disturb' sign and hoping it won't blow away with the first strong wind. But here's the reassuring part: You can anchor it firmly. Use clear, assertive communication. This doesn't mean being aggressive or confrontational. It's about being honest. For example, suppose you decide you don't want to discuss a certain painful topic. In that case, you might say, "I appreciate your concern, but I'm uncomfortable discussing that subject. Let's talk about something else." Remember, setting boundaries isn't about controlling others but managing your own interactions. People aren't mind readers; they'll often cross lines simply because they need to know where they are drawn. Setting and communicating your boundaries not only creates a safe and respectful space for yourself and others but also empowers you to take control of your relationships.

Respecting others' boundaries is just as crucial as establishing your own. It's a reciprocal process that enhances mutual respect and understanding in any relationship. Pay attention to verbal and nonverbal cues that might signal you're venturing too close to someone else's line. If a friend changes the subject when certain topics arise, they're setting a boundary, and it's your cue to steer clear of those waters. Respecting these signals without pushing or questioning further builds trust and shows that you value their comfort as much as your own.

Navigating the complex waters of relationships with well-defined and communicated boundaries makes communication much more straightforward. Understanding and implementing these principles allows for healthier interactions and more meaningful connections with family, friends, or colleagues. As you continue to explore and adjust your boundaries, remember they are not walls keeping the world out but gates that allow you to interact on your terms.

Dealing with Conflict: Strategies for Resolution

View conflict as a challenge requiring intelligence and emotional agility. Reframing conflict this way can transform it from a dreaded encounter into an opportunity for personal growth and deeper understanding. It's like finding a hidden level in a video game; you get a chance to test your skills, learn new strategies, and perhaps even gain unexpected rewards. Approaching conflict with this mindset encourages you to engage rather than avoid, to learn rather than win.

When you find yourself in conflict, your first tool is negotiation and dialogue in pursuit of a resolution. Effective negotiation involves understanding your needs and the other person's perspective. It's like being a detective and a diplomat rolled into one. Start by clearly stating your perspective and the outcome you hope for, then invite the other party to do the same. This sets the stage for open communication and shows you're committed to finding a solution that respects both sides. Finding common ground is crucial; it bridges troubled waters, allowing you to progress from confrontation to cooperation. Perhaps you both value honesty in your interactions or share similar goals but differ in your methods. Highlighting these shared values and objectives can turn the tide of the conversation, steering it towards constructive outcomes rather than a standoff.

However, even the most skillful negotiators can find themselves over their heads. If neither party is willing to budge, consider asking a neutral third party to step in as a mediator—someone you both trust. It's crucial to keep the communication lines clear and the emotional volume at a moderate level to prevent a conflict from escalating. One effective strategy is using "I" statements rather than "you" accusations, which can sound like blame and ignite defensive responses. For example, saying, "I feel overlooked when I'm not included in the decision-making process," is less confrontational than "You never consider my opinion!"

Additionally, keep an eye on non-verbal cues. A clenched jaw or averted eyes can communicate volumes. If you notice the conversation heating up, suggest a brief pause—sometimes, a few moments of cooling off can prevent the dialogue from boiling over.

After the dust has settled, whether the conflict was resolved smoothly or left a few scratches, the post-conflict phase is your chance to cement gains or repair damages. This is when reflection turns into action. Discuss ways to implement the agreed-upon solutions if the conflict leads to a resolution. This might involve setting up follow-up meetings or dividing responsibilities. If the conflict ended in a stalemate or with frayed nerves, consider reaching out to mend fences. A simple message expressing your willingness to move forward positively can pave the way for future interactions. It's also beneficial to review the conflict internally. What did you learn? How could you handle similar situations better in the future? This reflective practice prepares you for future conflicts. It contributes to your growth as a communicator and a leader in your personal and professional life.

Navigating the complex dynamics of conflict with grace and effectiveness isn't just about preserving relationships—it's about enriching them. View conflict as an opportunity to practice negotiating and finding common ground, preventing escalation, and taking thoughtful steps afterward. Following this strategy can transform potential battles into building blocks for more robust, resilient connections.

Building Strong Friendships in Adulthood

Making new friends in adulthood can seem daunting, but expanding your social circle after school can also be an adventure. Friends enrich your life and inspire you. Begin by leveraging your interests; if you enjoy reading, join a local book club; if you are artistic, enroll in a pottery or painting class. Join a sports club or invite a few colleagues to watch a movie or go for a meal together. Aim to turn invitations down only if you have no choice because each interaction could be the beginning of a new friendship. The key is to show up consistently. Regular attendance strengthens acquaintances into friendships.

Moreover, be proactive; don't wait for others to make the first move. Extend a coffee invitation post-workout or suggest a group hangout after class. Remember, everyone's apprehensive about reaching out, so your initiative might be just the nudge others need.

Now, let's talk about deepening those new friendships into rooted connections. Here's where shared experiences and vulnerability play pivotal roles. Plan activities that go beyond the usual hangouts. Road trips, hiking adventures, or even tackling a community service project together can create shared memories and deepen bonds. During these experiences, open up about your aspirations, fears, and experiences. Vulnerability is a two-way street; as you open up, it invites others to share their narratives, allowing for a deeper emotional connection. It's like peeling back layers to reveal the core of your personality, which fosters a stronger, more genuine friendship. But remember, vulnerability should be paced and reciprocal. Gauge how much others share and gradually open up to ensure everyone's comfort.

Balancing these friendships with life's myriad other commitments can sometimes feel like juggling flaming torches. It's about prioritizing quality over quantity. You don't need a sprawling network of friends to feel socially fulfilled; a few close friendships can be just as satisfying. Schedule regular meet-ups, but be flexible. Life can be unpredictable, and sometimes, an understanding text saying, "Let's raincheck to a day when you're less swamped," can be as bonding as a night out. Use technology to your advantage; a quick text or a meme can keep the connection warm, even when you're drowning in deadlines. It's about maintaining that contact thread, no matter how thin, until you can weave it back into a stronger connection.

Lastly, consider how friendships not only enrich your life but also contribute to your personal growth. Friends often act as mirrors, reflecting aspects of ourselves we might overlook. They can inspire us to change, grow, and take risks we might not dare to take otherwise. Moreover, they provide support through life's inevitable shifts—career changes, moves, relationships, and personal milestones. Recognizing and appreciating these roles can deepen your appreciation for these relationships, encouraging you to invest more heart and energy into them. As you and your friends grow together, these relationships can become integral parts of your life's framework, supporting you, lifting you, and enriching your journey in ways you might never have anticipated.

Navigating the complexities of adult friendships requires intention, effort, and a bit of courage. But the rewards—deep, supportive, and enriching connections—are worth the investment. As you continue to meet new people, deepen existing connections, balance your social life with personal duties, and grow alongside your friends, you'll find that these relationships are invaluable threads in the fabric of your adult life, adding layers of joy, support, and color to your everyday existence.

Romantic Relationships: Red Flags and Compatibility

Navigating romantic relationships can often feel like sailing without a compass, thrilling yet bewildering. Understanding the signs of trouble (red flags) and harmony (compatibility factors) is crucial for a fulfilling relationship. Let's start by spotting those red flags. They are not just minor disagreements about which movie to watch. Red flags are more serious indicators that the relationship might have unhealthy dynamics. For instance, if your significant other frequently dismisses your feelings or opinions, it's a red flag waving right in front of you. This behavior can escalate into a pattern where your self-esteem starts to erode, which can be a destructive trend.

Another glaring red flag is jealousy. Incessant texting whenever you're apart. This kind of jealousy can suffocate a relationship. It's rooted in insecurity and control, not love and trust. Then there's the issue of communication—or, should I say, the lack of it? If you're getting the silent treatment every time things get a bit rocky, or if every attempt at a serious conversation turns into a circus act of evasion, it's not just frustrating; it's a bright red flag. Effective communication underpins the foundations of any healthy relationship; without it, you're just two people occupying the same space, not truly connected.

Now, let's talk about what makes two people click beyond shared hobbies or a mutual love for horror movies. Core values are the anchor here. If you value honesty above all else and your partner has a more, let's say, 'flexible' approach to the truth, you're likely to run into problems. Similarly, suppose independence is your mantra, but your partner prefers a more enmeshed way of living. In that case, it's going to create tension. Understanding and sharing core values can foster a deep connection that weathers mundane squabbles and more serious arguments.

Communication styles also play a critical role in compatibility. If you're someone who needs to talk through issues and feelings as they arise, but your partner is more of a 'process internally and discuss later' kind of person, finding a rhythm that respects both styles is crucial. This means you can still mirror each other perfectly but understand and adapt to each other's communication needs.

Life goals are the compass guiding your long-term compatibility. These include career ambitions, opinions on marriage, and thoughts on children. Imagine you are dead set on a nomadic lifestyle, working remotely from a different country every year, but your partner dreams of a quiet suburban life with a stable job and kids. With alignment and compromise on these big-ticket items, the relationship might be able to find a lasting direction. Discussing these goals early on is crucial, not when you're already deep into planning a future that might need to align.

Managing a breakup can sometimes be frightening, but it is something we are likely to experience at some stage. Ending a relationship, especially one intertwined with your daily life and dreams, can feel like pulling away from a part of yourself. Yet, it's important to approach this with dignity and self-care. Recognize when a relationship no longer serves your well-being or aligns with your path. Communicate openly about your feelings and reasons without blame or bitterness. If your romantic partner breaks up with you, don't try to hold on to someone who no longer wants to be with you. Let them go. Maintain your pride and dignity. Take time to grieve, to heal, and to rediscover your individuality. Surround yourself with support, immerse yourself in your hobbies, and allow yourself the space to reflect on what you've learned from the experience. This isn't just about ending a chapter; it's also about growth and setting the stage for whatever comes next. Move on.

As you navigate romantic relationships' complexity, remember that understanding red flags, compatibility, and the right approach to breakups can transform your experiences from bewildering to enlightening. You're equipped to get through a breakup with the proper knowledge and tools.

Networking: Creating Valuable Professional Relationships

Networking might include swapping business cards or adding connections on LinkedIn as if they were collectible stickers. It's a vital strategy in your career growth. Connecting with professionals in your field opens the door to potential job opportunities, building a network of support, inspiration, and mutual benefits. These connections can turn into mentorships, partnerships, or job leads. Plus, each positive interaction adds a layer of confidence and satisfaction to your professional persona, boosting your workplace happiness and reducing the feeling of being just another cog in the machine.

Making the most of networking opportunities starts with being prepared. Know the terrain. Before attending networking events or reaching out online, do your homework. Research the people you want to connect with. Understand their roles, projects, and interests. This preparation makes you look informed and helps tailor your conversations to resonate with their professional landscapes. At events, be the person with a smile, a firm handshake, and an engaging opening line. Instead of the worn-out, "So, what do you do?", try sparking conversations with something more dynamic like, "What projects are you excited about right now?" It shows genuine interest and sets the stage for a meaningful exchange rather than just a transactional badge scan.

Leveraging social media smartly is another crucial strategy. Platforms such as LinkedIn aren't just for job hunting but also for building relationships. Share relevant articles, comment on posts by industry leaders, or publish your insights. This activity elevates your visibility and shows you're engaged and knowledgeable. But remember, the goal is to build authentic connections, not just a hefty list of contacts. Quality trumps quantity every time. A hundred superficial connections look good on your profile, but ten solid relationships will likely prove much more beneficial. These connections will vouch for you, share their expertise, and introduce you to others in their trusted circles.

Authentic connections are the framework for effective networking. Networking involves a give-and-take attitude. Always think about how you can add value to your connections. Can you offer unique insights, help with a project, or make an introduction? This reciprocity makes the relationship mutually beneficial and much more likely to develop into a strong professional bond. It's like being part of a club where everyone looks out for one another. Regular check-ins can keep these relationships vibrant and healthy. A quick message asking about a project they mentioned or sharing an article you think they'd find interesting keeps you on their radar positively. It shows you care about the relationship beyond what it can bring you professionally.

Maintaining professional relationships requires effort. Continuous engagement and mutual support help these relationships grow and flourish. Celebrate your contacts' successes, offer support during challenges, and remain a positive, proactive presence in their professional lives. This ongoing engagement ensures that your network remains a dynamic asset, full of individuals who respect and value your connection.

As we wrap up this exploration of networking, remember that the roots of rewarding professional relationships are often found in genuine interactions, mutual respect, and shared growth. Approaching networking with a strategy emphasizing authenticity and reciprocal value sets you up for a flourishing career filled with robust professional relationships. These connections advance your career goals and enhance your emotional well-being, making your professional journey successful and satisfying. As you continue to weave these connections through your career, you'll find that your professional life becomes more prosperous and nuanced, full of opportunities and shared successes.

As we close this chapter on building robust professional and personal relationships, remember the power of communication, boundary-setting, conflict management, and genuine connections in creating a fulfilling life. Each interaction and relationship is a thread in the intricate tapestry of your life. Nurture them with care, and watch as your world becomes richer in every sense.

In the next chapter, we explore another vital aspect of adulting: navigating the digital landscape. Here, we'll unravel the complexities of maintaining your digital identity and relationships in an increasingly online.

Notes

Make a Difference

Unlock the Power of Generosity

"We make a living by what we get, but we make a life by what we give."

— Winston Churchill

Hey there, amazing reader!

Thank you for diving into **Life Skills for Young Adults**. We've been on quite the journey together, tackling everything from financial freedom to building resilience and finding career success. Now, I have a small favor to ask that could make a big impact.

Would you help someone you've never met, even if you never got credit for it?

Imagine a young adult, just like you, standing at the crossroads of life, looking for guidance. They're eager to learn, grow, and make a difference, but they're not sure where to start. That's where this book comes in, and that's where you come in.

Our mission is to make **Life Skills for Young Adults** accessible to everyone. We believe that by sharing practical advice, personal stories, and easy-to-follow strategies, we can help young adults everywhere achieve financial security, emotional resilience, and career success.

But here's the deal: most people judge a book by its cover and its reviews. Your review can be the beacon of hope for someone in need of direction.

Your review can help ...

- One more small business owner to support their community.
- One more budding entrepreneur to take the leap.
- One more job seeker to find meaningful work.
- One more person to transform their life.
- One more dream to become a reality.

It takes less than 60 seconds.

Could you leave a review?

Click the link below to leave your review:

If you feel good about helping out another young adult, you're in good company. You're one of us. Together, we're building a community that supports one another through every challenge and triumph.

Thank you from the bottom of my heart. I'm thrilled to help you conquer life's challenges and achieve your dreams faster than you ever thought possible. The best is yet to come in the following chapters.

Your biggest fan, SquareRoets

Is this perhaps a friend in need?

P.S. Fun fact: Helping others not only feels great, but it also makes you more valuable to them. If you know someone who could benefit from this book, why not share it with them? Let's spread the knowledge and support one another!

5
Pathways to Professional Fulfilment

> *"Success is not the key to happiness. Happiness is the key to success. If you love what you are doing, you will be successful."*
>
> — Albert Schweitzer

Welcome to the thrilling adventure of professional life, where many paths wait to be explored. In this chapter, we are looking at how to thrive and find your path, and maybe even have a chance to appreciate life. Think of this book as your tool for carving out a clear, fulfilling career path that resonates with who you are and what you love. The journey ahead is filled with excitement and possibilities, and we're here to guide you every step of the way.

Discovering Your Passion: Self-Assessment Tools

Identifying Interests

Imagine each of your interests as a glowing spark. Some might flicker softly—a mild curiosity about astronomy or a fleeting fascination with French cinema. Others burn more brightly, like a longstanding passion for painting or coding. The trick is to recognize and gather these sparks to illuminate your career path. Here's where self-assessment tools come into play, empowering you to take control of your career journey.

Start with personality tests like the Myers-Briggs Type Indicator or the Strong Interest Inventory. These can provide insights into your personality traits and their alignment with various career options. For something more dynamic, try mind mapping. Use a notepad, write down activities that engage and energize you at the center, and then branch out with related skills or professions. This visual brainstorming can illuminate connections between your interests and potential career paths you might not have considered. For instance, a love for storytelling could branch into writing, marketing, or even game design careers. Your interests don't have to exist in isolation; they can come together in various combinations, leading you to a potential job that can bring satisfaction and joy.

* * *

Values and Skills Alignment

Ideally, your core values and skills should align with your job. Clarity about your values and skills is crucial to avoid a misfit. Reflect on what matters most to you. Is it creativity, stability, influence, or autonomy? Identifying these values serves as your compass, reassuring you that you're on the right path and guiding your career decisions toward roles that resonate with your principles.

Simultaneously, conduct a frank assessment of your skills. Which are you good at, and more importantly, which do you enjoy using? Sometimes these overlap, but not always. You might be good at math but thrilled by graphic design. Tools such as skills assessments or even feedback from past educators or employers can help you gauge where your strengths lie. The sweet spot for career satisfaction is where your values and skills intersect with the market's needs. Finding this intersection can propel you into a career that feels less like work and more like a paid hobby.

Career Exploration Resources

Venturing into the career exploration phase without resources can be overwhelming. Can you imagine yourself trying to find treasure without a treasure map? Thankfully, the map is readily available and rich with details. Start with online platforms like LinkedIn, Glassdoor, or Indeed, which can offer insights into various industries, companies, and job roles. These platforms are like your GPS, offering routes and real-time traffic updates through company reviews and job postings.

Informational interviews are your off-road excursions. You can contact professionals in your field of interest and ask for a chat over coffee or a virtual meet-up. These conversations can offer invaluable insights you won't find in any brochure or website. They provide a candid look at the day-to-day realities of a profession, the challenges faced, and the skills truly necessary for the job.

Long-term Goal Setting

Long-term career goals are more than just aspirations; they're your roadmap to success. They give you direction and motivation, but setting your goals smartly is the key. Ensure they are Specific, Measurable, Achievable, Relevant, and Time-bound (SMART). Instead of vaguely aiming to 'be successful,' define what success looks like for you. Is it becoming a head designer at a major tech firm in five years? Or launching your own startup by the age of 30? These goals are your checkpoints on the map of your professional journey. They're ambitious, yes, but also clear and structured, making the path to achieving them navigable and the progress measurable.

Navigating the thrilling, sometimes intimidating paths of professional fulfillment is an adventure in itself. It requires self-knowledge, strategic planning, and a bit of bold exploration. But with the right tools and resources, you're well-equipped to carve out a career that's not only successful on paper but deeply satisfying. As you continue to explore and apply these strategies, remember that every step, decision, and pivot is crafting a career uniquely yours, aligning with your passions, utilizing your skills, and honoring your values.

Exploring Career Paths: Interviews with Professionals

Informational interviews are like having a map that doesn't just show the treasure chest but also details the terrain—what skills are golden, which paths are tricky, and what challenges you might face. So, let's break down how to navigate these rich resources, transform casual chats into treasure troves of insight, and network like a pro without awkwardness.

Gathering Insights

Informational interviews are gold mines for firsthand insights about work life. They offer a peek behind the curtain of glamorous job descriptions and reveal daily life in various professions. This is your chance to ask burning questions like, 'What does a typical day look like in your role?' or 'What do you love and find challenging about your job?' These aren't just inquiries; they're your way of scanning the professional landscape, identifying if a particular career path aligns with your expectations and lifestyle preferences. It's one thing to admire the glossy surface of a career from afar and quite another to understand the nuts and bolts that hold it together. These sessions can help you discern if a job's daily grind sounds like something you can see yourself tackling.

Preparing Questions

Now, onto crafting meaningful questions. You don't have to stick to a script. Still, you do have to be curious about the details, and prepared questions will help you lead the dialogue to gather as much information as possible. Start with broad questions to set a comfortable pace, then gradually drill down to specifics. For instance, after discussing a typical day, pivot to asking, "What skills are crucial for success in this role?" or "How do you see this industry evolving over the next few years?" Each question should peel back a layer, revealing more about the realities of the job and the industry at large. Also, consider queries about company culture, work-life balance, and advancement opportunities. These questions can reveal if a potential work environment will be nurturing or stifling for your growth. Think of it as gathering information to make an informed career decision.

Networking Opportunities

Let's demystify networking in this context—it's not about schmoozing or handing out business cards like flyers. It's about building genuine connections. Each informational interview is a networking goldmine. You're not just gathering information; you're also making an impression. Approach these interactions with professionalism and genuine interest. If you resonate with the person you're interviewing, express your appreciation and interest in keeping in touch. A simple follow-up email thanking them for their time can open doors to future conversations. Remember, people are more likely to assist someone they've interacted positively with. So, make each meeting count by being attentive, respectful, and engaging. Over time, these connections can evolve into mentorships or even spark opportunities like job referrals.

Analyzing Information

After each interview, take the time to reflect and analyze the information gathered. This isn't just about taking notes but connecting the dots. How does what you've learned align with your career aspirations, desired lifestyle, and values? Use this analysis to refine your career goals or pivot directions if a particular revelation strikes a chord. For instance, if multiple professionals mention the importance of coding skills in your dream industry, and you have none, it might be time to consider relevant courses. Or, if you discover an aspect of the industry that doesn't sit well with your values, it might prompt you to explore related fields instead. This reflective process ensures that the insights you gain actively inform your career strategy, helping you build a path that leads to professional success and personal fulfillment.

By effectively leveraging informational interviews, you're not just passively observing the professional world but actively engaging with it and sculpting your future. Each conversation is a step closer to a career that excites and suits you. So, keep asking, keep learning, and, most importantly, keep connecting. You never know when you will need those connections.

The Role of Internships: Gaining Real-World Experience

Think of internships as your personal sneak peek into the backstage of the industry you're training to enter. Internships provide valuable real-world experience that is often unattainable in classroom settings. They help you understand the practical applications of your studies and give you a clearer picture of what daily life in your chosen field looks like. More than that, they can be your golden ticket into your desired industry, offering a foot in the door at companies that might otherwise seem like fortresses to break into.

Internships allow you to apply academic theories in real work environments, test your skills and adaptability, and learn directly from seasoned professionals. They often challenge you to step out of your academic comfort zone and handle tasks that require quick thinking and problem-solving, providing a rigorous test drive of your potential career path. Imagine being part of a team working on a critical project, your ideas taking shape and contributing to tangible outcomes. This boosts your confidence and enriches your resume with practical experience, making you a more attractive candidate to future employers. If you make an excellent impression, they might make you an offer to join the company after your studies.

Finding Internships

Securing the right internship starts with knowing where to look and how to apply strategically. Begin with your university's career center, which can offer a wealth of resources, including exclusive listings and recruitment events where you can connect directly with employers. Please pay attention to online job boards and company websites; they often list internship opportunities for students and recent graduates. You can use networking to advance in your search for an internship. Reach out to alums from your school who are working in your field of interest. LinkedIn can be particularly useful for this, allowing you to connect with professionals and even search for mutual links who might be able to introduce you.

When applying, tailor your application to each internship. Generic applications are easy to spot and often don't pass the first review round. Ensure that you emphasize the skills and experiences you feel are most relevant to the internship you are applying for. Demonstrate your knowledge about the company and its industry. This shows genuine interest and initiative, qualities that are highly attractive to potential employers. Your ultimate goal is to stand out from the crowd. You want to avoid blending in with a sea of applicants.

Maximizing the Internship Experience

Once you land an internship, the real work begins—not just the work you're assigned but the work of making the most out of every opportunity. Treat your internship as a prolonged job interview and a learning opportunity. Show initiative by asking for more responsibilities and seeking out projects that allow you to showcase your skills and dedication. Be proactive about learning; ask questions, seek feedback, and absorb as much knowledge as possible. Building relationships is also crucial. Connect with colleagues and supervisors, attend professional events, and make your presence known and positive. You will be grateful for these connections as you advance in your career. They can offer guidance, recommendations, and potential job leads.

Transitioning from Internship to Employment

Turning an internship into a full-time job is like turning a trial run into a victory lap, but it requires strategy and professionalism. Throughout your internship, demonstrate your value to the company through your hard work, creativity, and teamwork. As the end of your internship approaches, express your interest in continuing to work with the organization. Schedule a meeting with your supervisor to discuss your performance and potential employment opportunities. Even if a job offer isn't immediately available, staying in touch with your colleagues and supervisors can open doors later. Send periodic updates about your professional growth and new qualifications, and keep an eye on open positions at the company.

Internships are more than resume fillers or educational requirements; they are a critical stepping-stone to full-time employment and a successful career. By strategically choosing, securing, and maximizing your internships, you gain invaluable real-world experience and set the stage for a seamless transition into the professional world. Whether it leads directly to a job offer or paves the way for future opportunities, each internship is a crucial component of your own professional development, which will equip you with the skills, experiences, and connections necessary to flourish in your chosen field.

Crafting a Winning Resume and Cover Letter

Think of your resume and cover letter as your personal marketing agent. How do you ensure your documents make a potential employer take notice and want to know more about you?

Resume Essentials

Your resume is more than just a list of jobs and schools. It's a carefully crafted narrative that showcases your most relevant experiences, skills, and accomplishments. Start with a clear header with your name, phone number, and professional email address—"partylover123" won't impress. Next, a sharp, engaging summary captures your professional persona's essence. Think of it as your elevator pitch; in two to three sentences, highlight your significant achievements and the unique value you bring to the table.

Now, dive into the meat of the matter—your experience section. This isn't just a chronology of your job titles; it's your chance to shine. For each position, list your title, the company's name, and the timeframe you were there. Underneath, in bullet points, detail your responsibilities, but focus on accomplishments that quantify your impact. Did you increase sales, improve efficiency, or lead a project? Quantify it. "Led a team that increased sales by x%" sounds much more impressive than "Responsible for managing a team."

Education comes next. If you're freshly out of school, place this section before your professional experience. Include your degree, the institution's name, and graduation year. If you have higher education or relevant certifications, those go here too. Skills, especially technical ones relevant to the job, should be clearly listed—think of them as keywords that make your resume searchable. And please, let's leave out 'proficient in Microsoft Word'—it's 2024, and that's like saying you can use a toaster.

Cover Letter Strategy

While your resume is all about the facts, your cover letter is where your personality comes into play. This isn't the place for a regurgitation of your resume. Instead, it's your opportunity to tell a story, explain why you're passionate about the job, and why you'd be a fantastic fit. Start with how you found the job and why it excited you. Then, pick a couple of essential experiences from your resume and dive deeper. Tell the story of how you tackled a problem, led a team under pressure, or learned a crucial skill. You must keep it short and to the point. It must keep the reader's interest.

Your cover letter should complement your resume, not be a mere copy of it. Suppose your resume says you're great at leading projects. In that case, your cover letter should show a specific example of that leadership in action. Wrap up by stating how you look forward to contributing to the company and inviting them to review your resume for more details. Oh, and a pro tip: address the letter to a real person. "Dear Hiring Manager" is so impersonal. A quick LinkedIn search can turn up the name of the recruiter or HR manager.

Customization for Each Application

Tailoring your resume and cover letter for each application might sound like a chore. Still, each job and company has its own culture and needs. Your task is to adjust your documents to meet these specifics. Mirror the language of the job ad, focus on the experiences most relevant to the position, and always make sure your documents speak directly to the requirements listed by the employer. This level of customization shows that you've taken the time to craft a thoughtful, targeted application.

Common Mistakes to Avoid

Typos and grammatical errors are the quickest way to damage your credibility. They scream, "I didn't bother proofreading this." Have someone else review your documents before you send them off. Another common blunder is being overly humble. Your resume and cover letter are not the places for modesty. If you excelled, say so.

Conversely, over-fluffing your achievements can be just as damaging. Stay honest—stretching the truth can come back to bite you, especially in an era where background checks are standard. Lastly, avoid generic descriptors like 'hardworking' and 'team player.' Show, don't tell. Provide concrete examples demonstrating these qualities in action, making your claims believable and your documents compelling.

Creating a winning resume and cover letter is like dressing for the job interview every day you're on the job hunt. Ensure every detail, from the layout to the content, is polished, professional, and poised to impress. With these tools at your disposal, you're ready to make a striking first impression that will pave the way to job interview invitations. So, go forth, tailor meticulously, and prepare to land your dream job.

Ace the Interview: Techniques and Tips

Job interviews can be exhilarating, nerve-wracking, and sometimes downright bewildering. However, with proper preparation and the right attitude, you can transform this daunting challenge into an impressive display of your capabilities. Let's unpack the strategies to make you the star of your next job interview, turning potential stumbling blocks into stepping stones for success.

* * *

Preparation is Key

Imagine entering an interview knowing the company's name, culture, recent achievements, and challenges. This isn't just preparation; it's arming yourself with knowledge that can set you apart from the sea of candidates. Start by diving deep into the company's website, absorbing everything from its mission statement to quarterly reports. LinkedIn and other social media platforms can offer insights into the company's current projects and those driving them. This knowledge allows you to provide tailored answers to align with the company's goals and showcase how you can contribute to their success.

Practicing your answers is like rehearsing for a big performance. Questions like "What are your strengths and weaknesses?" or "Where do you see yourself in five years?" should not catch you off-guard. Craft thoughtful, genuine answers and rehearse them, but not to the point where they sound memorized. Use a mirror or run mock interviews with a friend or mentor who can provide feedback. This preparation doesn't just ease your nerves; it polishes your delivery, ensuring your responses are confident and natural.

Presenting Yourself

First impressions are potent, and your appearance and demeanor set the tone in an interview before you even speak. Think of your attire as the cover of your personal book—it should be appealing, appropriate, and aligned with the company's culture. Whether business formal or smart casual, your clothes should fit well and be in mint condition. But your presentation extends beyond clothes. Your body language speaks volumes. A firm handshake, a warm smile, and eye contact can communicate confidence and sincerity. Sit upright but relaxed, and be mindful of nervous tapping your foot or fidgeting with a pen. These small details can influence the vibe of the entire interview. You need to appear composed and assured.

Answering Tough Questions

Every interview has that moment—the curveball question that seems to probe into the depths of your soul, testing your mettle. Whether addressing a gap in your resume, discussing a past failure, or handling a complex hypothetical situation, the key is to remain calm and thoughtful. Structure your answers using the STAR method (Situation, Task, Action, Result) to provide clear, concise, and organized responses. For instance, if asked about a project that didn't go as planned, outline the situation, your role, the actions you took to address the problems, and the outcomes. This method clarifies your thought process and demonstrates your problem-solving and critical-thinking skills.

Follow-Up Etiquette

The interview might be over, but your opportunity to impress is still being determined. Sending a thank-you email within 24 hours reflects your professionalism and enthusiasm for the position. Personalize this note by referencing specific moments from the interview that were insightful or particularly enjoyable. This shows that you were engaged and reinforces your interest in the role. A polite follow-up email is appropriate if you have yet to hear back within the expected timeframe. It can reiterate your interest and inquire about the timeline for a decision. Remember, persistence is vital, but patience is a virtue. Bombarding the hiring manager with daily emails won't win you any points.

Mastering these interview techniques can significantly enhance your chances of making a lasting impression and securing the job. From thorough preparation and polished presentation to skillful answering and thoughtful follow-up, each element plays a crucial role in demonstrating your professionalism, suitability, and enthusiasm for the role. Now, equipped with these strategies, confidently step into your next interview, ready to showcase your talents and charm your potential employers.

Navigating Your First Job: Expectations vs Reality

The leap from the structured world of academia to the dynamic arena of professional life is exhilarating yet fraught with curveballs. Adjusting your expectations to this new reality is crucial for surviving and thriving in your newfound role.

Adjusting to Professional Life

Imagine this: one day, you're a student with a somewhat flexible schedule, and the next, you're expected to hit the ground running in a 9-to-5 job (or, let's be honest, sometimes 8-to-6). The transition can be jarring. It's vital to set realistic expectations right from the start. Understand that, unlike school, where grades directly reflect your effort, the work environment values results and processes. Success might not come from acing a test but from how effectively you manage projects, communicate with team members, or handle feedback. Initially, focus on learning the ropes. Observe, ask questions, and absorb as much as you can. Remember, it's okay to feel overwhelmed at first—every seasoned professional was once a rookie.

Professional Etiquette

Navigating workplace etiquette is like learning a new dance. Every company has its rhythm and steps, whether it's the formality of communication or the unspoken rules of lunchroom politics. Key aspects include communication, punctuality, and teamwork. Communicating effectively in a professional setting often means being concise yet thorough. Whether it's emails or project updates, clarity and professionalism are paramount. Punctuality shows respect for other people's time—a non-negotiable trait in the professional world. It's not just about being on time but also about meeting deadlines and being reliable. Then there's teamwork. Even if you're more of a solo performer, understanding the dynamics of working in a team is crucial. It's about finding harmony in diversity, aligning your efforts with others, and sometimes, stepping back to let others lead. Mastering these steps can help you glide smoothly through your daily tasks and interactions.

Seeking Feedback and Growth Opportunities

One of the most proactive steps you can take in your new role is actively seeking feedback. Think of feedback as the GPS for your career path—it helps you navigate your journey, showing you where you're on track and where you might need to recalibrate. Approach feedback with openness and a mindset geared towards growth. Regular check-ins with your supervisor can be invaluable. Ask specific questions: "What aspects of my work are strong, and where can I improve?" Also, be on the lookout for opportunities to expand your skills. Whether it's a workshop, a cross-departmental project, or a new software tool, every new skill acquired is a stepping stone in your career advancement. Remember, growth often happens outside of comfort zones, so embrace challenges as opportunities to learn and evolve.

Work-Life Balance

Last but definitely not least, let's talk about maintaining a healthy work-life balance. It's tempting to throw yourself into your job, especially when you're new and eager to impress. However, remember that marathon runners pace themselves—they know that sprinting at full speed from the start is unsustainable. Set boundaries from the beginning. This might mean logging off from work emails after a certain hour or ensuring your weekends are work-free. Invest time in activities that recharge you, whether it's a hobby, exercise, or spending time with loved ones. A well-balanced life is good for your well-being and enhances your productivity and creativity at work.

Starting your first job is frightening and exciting, with the potential for discovery and growth. Set realistic expectations, master professional etiquette, actively seek feedback, and maintain a healthy work-life balance. These strategies will equip you to succeed as an employed professional in your new life.

As we close this chapter on navigating your first job, remember this is just the beginning of your career journey. Each challenge and triumph is a brushstroke in the broader canvas of your professional life. Ahead lies a world of opportunities to deepen your expertise, expand your horizons, and continue evolving personally and professionally.

Notes

6
Skills for the Modern Workplace

"In the modern workplace, the most successful individuals are those who are willing to learn and adapt."

— Unknown

Imagine stepping into a bustling city where the streets are paved with circuits and the buildings are made of cloud data. Welcome to the tech-driven world of the modern workplace, where digital literacy isn't just a flashy term you toss around at dinner parties—it's as essential as knowing how to tie your shoes. Gone are the days when 'computer skills' meant you could type a Word document without hunting for every key. Today, being tech-savvy means confidently navigating through apps, platforms, and digital tools.

Digital Literacy: Navigating Today's Tech-Driven World

Essential Digital Skills

In this digital age, specific skills are critical survival tools. Mastering basic software proficiency, whether it's the Microsoft Office Suite or Google's array of tools, empowers you to manipulate data, create visually engaging presentations, and confidently manage your daily tasks. Online communication tools such as Slack, Zoom, and Teams have become the new workplace locales. Navigating these platforms ensures you're not that person who accidentally shares a meme in a professional chat or struggles to find the mute button during an entire meeting. This mastery gives you a sense of control in the digital landscape.

In today's job market, understanding the basics of content management systems (CMS) or customer relationship management (CRM) software can set you apart. These tools are many companies' backstage heroes, helping streamline processes and enhance customer interactions. By getting comfortable with these technologies, you're not just doing your job but optimizing it.

Staying Updated

The digital world is constantly evolving, and what's trending today might be obsolete tomorrow. Staying updated is not just necessary; it's a proactive approach to your career. Regularly setting time aside to learn about the latest software updates or exploring new tools your industry is buzzing about is a vital part of this. Online courses like Coursera, Udemy, or LinkedIn Learning can be your go-to trainers. They offer bite-sized lessons on everything from basic programming to advanced data analytics. Remember, in the race toward the future, learning is not a sprint but a marathon. Keeping pace requires consistent effort and curiosity; by being proactive, you can keep ahead of the curve.

Online Security Awareness

Knowing about cybersecurity is an essential asset. In a world where data breaches can topple giants, understanding the basics of online security—strong passwords, phishing scams, and secure internet practices—is crucial. It's like knowing how to lock your doors in a sketchy neighborhood. Educate yourself about security tools like two-factor authentication (2FA) or encrypted data storage options like VeraCrypt or BitLocker. 2FA adds an extra layer of security to your accounts by requiring a second verification form, such as a code sent to your phone. Encrypted data storage tools protect your sensitive information even if your device is lost or stolen. Protecting your personal and company data is about building trust and avoiding a disaster. When clients and colleagues know they can rely on you to safeguard information, your stock rises faster than tech shares in a bull market.

Leveraging Technology for Efficiency

Finally, let's harness the true power of technology—efficiency. Tools and apps designed to boost productivity are the secret weapons in your tech arsenal. Project management software like Asana, Trello, or Monday.com can transform you from a frazzled multitasker into a maestro of efficiency, orchestrating tasks and deadlines with the precision of a symphony conductor. Automation tools, such as Zapier or IFTTT, can take over repetitive tasks, freeing up your time to focus on work that requires a human touch—creativity, strategy, and personal interactions. These tools work by creating 'if this, then that 'rules and automating tasks like data entry, email responses, or social media posting. It's like having an army of robots at your disposal, each programmed to handle the mundane so you can target the extraordinary.

Navigating the tech-driven modern workplace can feel like something other than wandering through a labyrinth. With the right skills, a commitment to continuous learning, an awareness of cybersecurity, and the strategic use of technology, you're not just keeping up but setting the pace.

Time Management: Tools and Techniques for Efficiency

Imagine your day as a vast array of tasks, each demanding a portion of your time and energy. With a strategy, you might devote more attention to one and insufficient to another. Effective time management ensures you allocate just the right amount of time to each task, maximizing productivity without burning out. Let's discuss some useful time management techniques.

Prioritizing Tasks

Diving into your workday without a plan can be overwhelming. The key is to learn the art of prioritizing. Start by categorizing tasks using the Eisenhower Box—dividing your tasks into four categories: urgent and important, important but not urgent, urgent but not necessary, and neither urgent nor essential. This method acts like a filter, helping clarify which tasks you need to jump on immediately, which ones you can schedule for later, which ones you can delegate, and which ones you should drop. For instance, finishing a project due today? That's urgent and important. Signing up for a professional development workshop next month? Important, but not urgent. Checking your email for the tenth time before lunch? Perhaps urgent, but not essential. This approach clarifies your daily to-do list, aligns your efforts with your long-term goals, and ensures that each step you take is towards achieving something meaningful.

Scheduling and Planning

Once your tasks are prioritized, the next step is scheduling. This is where tools such as digital calendars and task managers become your best friends. Platforms like Google Calendar and Trello can transform your abstract to-do list into a structured schedule. Start by blocking time for your most energy-consuming tasks during your peak productivity hours—when you're feeling most capable and energetic. Remember to schedule breaks as well; they're not just free time—they're recovery periods that allow your brain to refresh and prepare for the next task. Incorporating these tools into your daily routine can help automate the planning process, making it less of a chore and more of a helpful habit. They can send reminders, prompt you to review and adjust your plan based on progress or setbacks and help keep everything neatly organized, from meetings to brainstorming sessions.

Avoiding Procrastination

Procrastination—the arch-nemesis of productivity. It's like the siren song that lures you away from your tasks with promises of temporary comfort, leaving you in dire straits later. Combatting procrastination begins with understanding why you're avoiding a task. Is it too boring, too complicated, or are you simply tired? Identifying the root cause can help find the right strategy to overcome it. The Pomodoro Technique requires that you work in focused sprints of 25 minutes followed by a 5-minute break. This method chops up your work into manageable intervals, making it less daunting and keeping your brain too engaged to seek distractions. Additionally, setting mini-deadlines for yourself throughout the day can create a sense of urgency that spurs action. Combine these with rewarding yourself for completing tasks—maybe a coffee break or a quick walk—and you'll find procrastination becoming a less frequent visitor.

Setting Boundaries

Effective time management allows you to achieve more in less time by creating boundaries that protect you from distractions and taking on too many commitments. You must learn to say no or not now, whether to colleagues asking for a 'quick favor' that isn't quick or to additional projects that you can't fit into your schedule without compromising your well-being. It also means setting boundaries with work hours to prevent burnout. Make it clear when you're at work and when you're at home, even if both happen in the same space. Use technology to support these boundaries—set 'Do Not Disturb' modes on your devices, use auto-responders to manage email expectations outside of work hours, and have a physical setup that allows you to physically 'close' your work area at the end of the day.

Mastering these time management tools and techniques transforms your workday from a whirlwind of tasks to a well-orchestrated symphony where each note plays at the right moment, creating a melody of productivity and balance. Whether you're a student juggling studies and part-time work, a rising professional navigating the corporate ladder, or an entrepreneur building a dream, these strategies are your keys to surviving and thriving in the whirlwind of life's responsibilities.

The Importance of Emotional Intelligence at Work

Some modern workplaces can feel frantic with everyone in motion and countless interactions occurring simultaneously. Being comfortable in such an environment requires more than just knowing the rules; you must also have emotional intelligence (EI). EI is the GPS that helps you steer through the complex dynamics of professional relationships smoothly and effectively. Understanding EI is like understanding the language of emotions—your own and those of others. It's an essential skill set comprising self-awareness, empathy, self-regulation, motivation, and social skills. These components work together like a well-oiled machine, enhancing your ability to navigate the workplace tactfully and confidently.

Self-awareness is the starting point. It requires tuning into your emotions, recognizing their impact on your thoughts and actions, and understanding how they affect others. Think of it as your psychologist: the better you understand your emotional triggers and the nuances of your mood swings, the better you can manage them. This internal clarity is crucial in a professional setting, where pressures can push your buttons in unexpected ways. Developing self-awareness can be as simple as keeping an emotion journal, where you jot down what you feel throughout the day and reflect on the triggers and responses. This habit sharpens your perception of your emotional landscape. It fortifies you against potential emotional upheavals that could throw you off your game.

Empathy can be described as your ability to put yourself in someone else's shoes, seeing the world through their eyes and understanding their emotions. This means tuning into your colleagues' feelings and perspectives in the workplace, which can significantly enhance your interactions and negotiations. It's the difference between a manager who barks orders, oblivious to the team's stress levels, and one who adjusts deadlines after sensing the team's overwhelming pressure. Developing empathy involves active listening—paying full attention to the speaker without mentally preparing your rebuttal. It also means being observant, noting what is said and how it is said, and responding with consideration. This skill turns everyday interactions into opportunities for connection and understanding, building a foundation of trust and respect.

Now, let's talk about EI in leadership. The best leaders aren't just visionaries but also people who understand emotions. They know how to inspire, motivate, and guide their teams through work life's emotional highs and lows. Emotional intelligence in leadership involves recognizing the emotional currents within the team and using that knowledge to manage attitudes and boost morale. For instance, during challenging times, an emotionally intelligent leader might share an inspiring story of a past challenge the team overcame, reigniting the team's confidence and focus. It's about more than just leading; it's about emotionally empowering the team, making the workplace not just a place of employment but a space of mutual growth and support.

Finally, let's consider EI's role in conflict resolution. Workplace conflicts are inevitable. However, handling them with emotional intelligence can transform these conflicts from office drama into catalysts for team cohesion and improvement. It starts with self-regulation—the ability to manage your emotions and remain calm under pressure. This self-control prevents conflicts from escalating by keeping emotional outbursts in check and maintaining a clear head for problem-solving. Then, using empathetic communication, you can address the root of the conflict without blame, focusing instead on understanding the perspectives involved and working towards a constructive resolution. This approach resolves the immediate issue and strengthens the team's ability to handle future conflicts, fostering a culture of openness and mutual respect.

Mastering emotional intelligence is like navigating a complex network of emotions and interactions. You need to develop self-awareness, empathy, and effective relationship management skills. In applying these leadership and conflict resolution skills, you equip yourself with the tools to survive in the modern workplace and thrive, making each professional interaction more meaningful and productive. As you continue to hone these skills, you'll find that they enhance your professional life and enrich your personal relationships, proving that emotional intelligence is a superpower in today's emotionally charged world.

Creative Problem-Solving and Innovation

In a world where every other resumé flaunts 'problem-solving skills', standing out in the workplace requires a dash of creativity and innovation. Think of creative problem-solving as seeing resources and solutions in places most people overlook. So, how do you turn your everyday thinking into a powerhouse of creativity and innovation? Let's discuss some ideas.

Fostering Creativity

Creativity in problem-solving requires an open-minded attitude. This means looking at problems from multiple angles rather than rushing toward the first solution that pops into your head. Take a page from the book 'Design Thinking,' which involves empathizing with users, defining the problem, ideating, creating prototypes, and testing. Applying this method encourages a deeper understanding of the problem at hand. It fosters innovative, effective, and user-centric solutions.

Encourage a brainstorming culture where no idea is too silly. Regular brainstorming sessions can be your idea incubators. Use techniques such as 'mind mapping,' where you visually plot out thoughts and connections around a central problem, or 'brainwriting,' where everyone writes their ideas down anonymously, allowing for uninhibited creativity. These methods generate numerous ideas and democratize the process, making every team member an active participant in problem-solving. Remember, creativity thrives in an atmosphere where ideas can bounce freely without the fear of judgment. So, keep these sessions light and playful—sometimes, the most off-the-wall idea can be the seed that grows into a groundbreaking solution.

Innovative Thinking Techniques

Let's explore techniques that can sharpen your innovative edge. Reverse engineering involves deconstructing successful products or systems to see how they work. Understanding these elements can spark ideas for solving your own challenges in novel ways. It's like disassembling a watch to learn how to build your own. Another technique is 'SCAMPER,' which stands for Substitute, Combine, Adapt, Modify, Put to another use, Eliminate, and Reverse (2020). Breaking down design thinking. Applying these verbs to problems helps you think outside the box and generate creative improvements. For instance, can you substitute a component for a cheaper one without losing functionality? Or, can you adapt a solution from another industry to fit your needs? Using SCAMPER can turn a standard problem-solving session into a creative powerhouse.

Implementing Solutions

Coming up with a creative solution is just the beginning. The real magic lies in bringing that idea to life. This phase involves making your ideas tangible, testing them in the real world, and refining them. Start with creating a prototype or a pilot version of your solution. It doesn't have to be perfect. The goal is to bring the abstract into the concrete—something you can see, touch, or use. For example, if your solution involves a new app feature, develop a basic version and see how it performs in a controlled group. Gather feedback on what works, what doesn't, and why. This feedback loop is crucial as it serves as the reality check for your creative aspirations, ensuring the solution is innovative but also practical and impactful.

Encouraging a Culture of Innovation

Lastly, you need the right ecosystem for creativity and innovation to thrive. This means fostering a workplace culture where innovation is encouraged and celebrated. Start by recognizing and rewarding creative efforts. Whether an idea succeeds or fails, the focus should be on the boldness of the attempt and the lessons learned. Create spaces that stimulate creativity. This could mean setting up brainstorming corners, having open spaces for spontaneous discussions, or ensuring a diverse team with varied skills and backgrounds to enhance creative friction. Organize 'hackathons' or 'idea marathons' where employees can dedicate time to solving company challenges with innovative solutions. These events can be fun, engaging, and a goldmine of fresh ideas.

You transform the mundane into a playground full of possibilities by embedding these practices into your daily work routine. Creative problem-solving and innovation become your way of thinking and operating, propelling you to be a standout problem-solver who can turn challenges into opportunities with a touch of creativity and a dash of innovation.

Leadership Skills for the Emerging Professional

Effective leaders are like chameleons, adept at adapting their style to meet their team's needs and the environment's demands. They're decisive yet flexible, authoritative yet approachable. However, these qualities don't just magically appear. They are honed through experience, reflection, and a conscious effort to grow.

Developing leadership qualities begins with a good, hard look in the mirror. Self-awareness is your first tool, starting with understanding your strengths and acknowledging your weaknesses. Are you great at seeing the big picture but sometimes overlook the details? Or maybe you're a wizard with numbers but freeze up when you need to deliver a presentation? Being able to recognize your positive traits allows you to leverage your strengths and work on your weaknesses. It's also about understanding your impact on others. How does your mood sway the team's morale? How do your communications shape the team's culture? Being mindful of these influences helps you sculpt your approach to leadership, ensuring that it is influential and inspiring.

Once you've mapped out your traits, the next step is to cultivate them deliberately. If decision-making isn't your forte, start small. Make quicker decisions on minor issues and observe the outcomes. If public speaking causes you unnecessary stress, seek opportunities to present in front of friendly audiences to build your confidence. Consider leadership workshops or mentoring sessions with established leaders you admire. These resources can provide you with valuable insights and actionable advice on refining your leadership style. Remember, becoming a leader isn't an overnight metamorphosis. It's a gradual evolution, marked by small victories and inevitable stumbles, each teaching you more about leading effectively.

Leading by Example

Now, let's talk about setting the pace. Leading by example is the foundation of effective leadership. Think about it—why would anyone on your team put in the extra effort if you clocked out early? Or adhere to protocols that you casually bypass? Setting high standards for yourself sets a benchmark for your team. It involves showing commitment, integrity, and enthusiasm. If you expect your team to be punctual, start by never being late. If quality is your mantra, double-check your work for errors. When your team sees you embodying the qualities you advocate, you earn their respect and inspire them to mirror these standards. It's about walking the talk every single day, without fail.

This approach extends beyond mere work habits. It encompasses how you handle stress, conflict, and failure. Suppose you can remain composed under pressure, deal with conflicts constructively, and learn from setbacks without pointing fingers. In that case, you're demonstrating resilience and accountability. These are powerful lessons for your team. They see these behaviors in action, understand their value, and integrate them into their own professional lives. Thus, leading by example isn't just about influencing the present; it's about imprinting on your team's future behavior.

Communication and Influence

Moving on to mastering the art of communication—it's the thread that ties your leadership qualities together. Effective communication is required to convey information while ensuring it's understood and embraced. It's a mix of clarity, empathy, and persuasion. Begin with being clear about your goals, expectations, and feedback. Ambiguity breeds confusion, and confusion hinders efficiency. Tailor your communication to your audience. What works for a boardroom presentation won't necessarily be effective in a casual team meeting. Listen actively to your team's ideas and concerns. This helps gather diverse insights and makes your team feel valued, fostering a cooperative rather than a confrontational workspace.

Then there's the aspect of influence. It's one thing to state your case but another to persuade others to come aboard. This requires a blend of logical reasoning, emotional appeal, and credibility. Whether pitching a new project or guiding your team through a change, how you present your message can make all the difference. Use stories, analogies, and examples that resonate with your team. Show enthusiasm and confidence in your proposals. People are naturally drawn to leaders who are passionate about their ideas and demonstrate a deep belief in their feasibility and success.

* * *

Delegating and Empowering

Finally, the true test of leadership lies in your ability to delegate and empower. Hoarding tasks burns you out and stunts your team's growth. Delegating shows trust in your team's abilities and encourages them to stretch their skills and take on new challenges. Start by matching tasks to people's strengths or developmental goals. Provide clear instructions and the necessary resources, then step back. Resist the urge to micromanage. Instead, be available to support and answer questions. This autonomy boosts your team's confidence and fosters a sense of ownership over their work.

Empowerment concerns encouraging lower-level decision-making, involving the team in problem-solving, and recognizing and acknowledging their contributions openly. Celebrate their successes and provide constructive feedback in private when areas need improvement. When your team feels empowered, they're more engaged, motivated, and committed to collective goals. They perceive that they are working with you to achieve a shared vision.

Mastering these leadership skills transforms you from a manager to a leader, from someone who merely oversees to someone who genuinely uplifts. It's about cultivating a leadership style that resonates authentically and fosters trust. It promotes growth for the individuals on your team and the enterprise as a whole. As you continue to refine these skills, remember that leadership is not just about directing others—it's about being a catalyst for change, a mentor for growth, and a beacon of integrity and inspiration.

The Basics of Project Management

Project management involves leading a team of individuals with diverse skills to attain a shared goal within set parameters and constraints.

Project Management Fundamentals

Project management encompasses three key phases: planning, execution, and monitoring. Planning is your roadmap. It involves setting clear objectives, defining the scope, and outlining the tasks needed to reach your goals—like sketching the blueprint of a building before laying the first brick. This phase requires you to think critically about what must be done, by whom, and when. Tools such as Gantt charts or Work Breakdown Structures can help visualize this plan, breaking down complex projects into manageable, actionable parts.

The next phase is execution. The plan means little if you can't translate it into action. This phase involves managing resources, directing activities, and ensuring the project team is engaged and motivated. It's the bustling construction site where the blueprint turns into reality. Effective leadership and clear communication are crucial to align with the project's ethos and keep all role players on track. Regular team meetings and updates help maintain momentum and promptly address issues that arise.

Monitoring is your ongoing reality check. It involves tracking the project's progress against the plan and adjusting as needed. Think of it as the feedback loop in your project's lifecycle. Using tools such as project dashboards and status reports, you can gauge if the project is on schedule, within budget, and aligned with the quality standards set during the planning phase. This continuous vigilance allows you to catch potential issues before they become full-blown problems, keeping the project on track toward completion.

Tools and Techniques

Software such as Microsoft Project, Asana, and Trello are particularly useful in the project management toolbox. These platforms offer features that streamline the three phases of project management. They enable you to assign tasks, set deadlines, update statuses, and communicate real-time changes. The beauty of these tools lies in their ability to keep everyone on the same page, which is crucial in managing complex projects with multiple moving parts and stakeholders.

Risk Management

Risk management is an essential component of any project. It concerns identifying what could go wrong, evaluating which risks might have the most impact, and establishing strategies to manage these risks effectively. Techniques such as SWOT analysis (Strengths, Weaknesses, Opportunities, and Threats) and risk mapping can help in this process. Prepare for the worst, but hope for the best. By ensuring risk mitigation strategies are in place, you can ensure your project remains resilient against uncertainty.

Team Collaboration

The heart of any project is its team. Fostering collaboration involves team members working together and creating a synergy where the whole is greater than the sum of its parts. This requires encouraging open communication, fostering trust, and promoting a team culture where every member feels valued and understood. Regular team-building activities can strengthen relationships, while tools such as shared workspaces or collaboration software can facilitate smooth interactions and information sharing. A team collaborating effectively can overcome complex challenges more efficiently and innovatively than any team member.

Navigating through the realms of project management requires you to be flexible yet focused and intuitive but organized. It's about seeing the big picture while managing the small details. As you continue to explore these strategies and tools, remember that each project is a learning opportunity. With each project, you'll refine your management skills and help your team members grow and succeed. This chapter was about teaching you to lead a team to achieve extraordinary results, creating a ripple effect of efficiency and innovation across your organization.

As this chapter closes, remember the harmonious blend of planning, execution, and monitoring in project management. Each element is crucial and requires your attention and skill. Keep honing these skills, and you'll find that managing even the most daunting projects can be achieved successfully.

Notes

7
Mastering Daily Life Tasks

"Great things are not done by impulse, but by a series of small things brought together."

— Vincent Van Gogh

As you step into adulthood, the art of cooking is a crucial skill to master. With a few basic skills in your arsenal, you'll navigate the kitchen with confidence and a sense of accomplishment.

* * *

Cooking Basics: Quick, Healthy Meals on a Budget

Meal Planning Made Simple

Meal planning, often seen as a mundane task, can actually be an exciting journey of culinary discovery. Set your course for the week ahead, and watch as your meals transform into a variety of categories that fit your lifestyle, adding excitement and efficiency to your grocery shopping.

Shopping with a list and buying ingredients in bulk for multiple meals not only saves money but also saves you from the stress of cooking every night. The freezer becomes your best friend, allowing you to cook in batches and freeze portions for those nights when you need a break from the kitchen.

Essential Cooking Techniques

Mastering a few basic techniques can turn the chore of cooking into a pleasant experience. Start with boiling—whether it's pasta, eggs, or potatoes, boiling is a fundamental skill you can't skip. Then, there's sautéing, perfect for those quick, flavorful dinners after a long day at work. A splash of oil, some chopped onions, a bit of garlic, and any veggies or proteins you have on hand, and voilà, you've got a meal that's out of this world.

Baking might not be on your daily to-do list, but it's a skill worth exploring. It requires patience but yields delightful, sweet (or savory) rewards. Start simple with dishes like roasted vegetables or a basic chicken tray bake. The beauty of baking is that the oven does most of the work, leaving you free to tackle other tasks or just relax.

Kitchen Essentials

Before you can cook, you need to equip your kitchen. Your essential toolkit consists of a chef's knife, a cutting board, a skillet, a saucepan, and a baking tray. These essentials will help you tackle most recipes without cluttering your kitchen with gadgets from infomercials that promise culinary stardom but rarely deliver.

As for ingredients, keep your pantry stocked with versatile staples like oils, spices, canned tomatoes, pasta, and rice. These are your building blocks for countless meals. Add fresh produce and proteins to your weekly shopping list, and you're ready to cook up a storm.

Recipes for Beginners

Now, armed with techniques and tools, let's put them to the test. Here's a simple, budget-friendly recipe to start your culinary journey: One-Pan Chicken and Veggie Bake. You'll need chicken breasts, assorted vegetables (think bell peppers, zucchini, and cherry tomatoes), olive oil, and your choice of herbs and spices. Toss everything onto a baking tray, drizzle with oil, sprinkle with herbs, salt, and pepper, and bake at 375°F (190°C) for about 25 minutes. This meal is forgiving, adaptable, and requires minimal supervision, making it a perfect launchpad for your cooking adventures.

Once you have mastered the basics, you can start simple and gradually expand your culinary repertoire. Remember, every great chef started with boiling water and burning a dish or two. The key is to keep experimenting, keep tasting, and enjoy the journey. Soon, you'll find that cooking is less of a daily chore and more of a creative outlet, a comforting ritual, and a delicious way to nourish body and soul.

Keeping It Clean: Simplified Housekeeping Strategies

Imagine the perfect living space, where your clothes are neatly folded in their drawers, books aligned on the shelf, and not a speck of dust anywhere. Sounds like a utopian dream? Well, it's closer to reach than you might think. With some simple daily cleaning habits, you can keep your living quarters habitable and immaculately organized. Let's start with the basics: daily habits that are easy to adopt and make a massive difference in maintaining a clean environment. It begins with making your bed every morning. Yes, it sounds trivial, but this simple act sets a tone of order for your day and instantly tidies up the look of your room. Next, adopt the 'clean as you go' mantra in the kitchen. Wash dishes or load the dishwasher right after eating; wipe down counters after meal prep. This habit prevents the daunting pile-up of chores and prepares your kitchen for its next culinary adventure.

But let's add a green twist to this—eco-friendly cleaning solutions. Why buy chemical-laden cleaners when you can whip up your own potions that are kind to the Earth and your wallet? For an all-purpose cleaner, mix equal parts white vinegar and water, add a squeeze of lemon for that zest of freshness, and pour it into a reusable spray bottle. This concoction can tackle everything from smudged windows to greasy stovetops. For tougher grime, baking soda is your best friend. Sprinkle it on, let it sit, scrub, and watch the magic happen. These natural solutions are effective and eliminate the risk of toxic chemicals lingering in your home. Plus, they can be a fun experiment in your very own kitchen lab, mixing and matching ingredients to find the perfect cleaning elixir.

Now, onto decluttering, an essential step in mastering the art of keeping a clean house. The rule here is simple: if you last used it a year ago, you don't need it. Start with your wardrobe—organize a fashion show for one, try everything on, and be ruthless in weeding out what doesn't fit or flatter. Apply similar tactics to books, gadgets, and even pantry items. Decluttering frees up space and reduces the time you spend cleaning and organizing down the road. It's about creating a space that feels open, airy, and light, where every item around you is there for a reason. Consider donating items that are still in good shape. This way, you're not just cleaning out your space but also contributing to a cycle of reuse that benefits the environment and those in need.

Finally, let's talk about creating organizational systems that stick. This isn't about overhauling your space with fancy gadgets and expensive bins. Sometimes, a simple shift in how you store things can make all the difference. Use drawer dividers for your clothes, assigning a specific spot for each category: socks in one compartment, shirts in another. Keep all your supplies in designated containers in your workspace and label them if necessary. For paperwork, adopt a filing system that works for you—be it digital or traditional. The key is consistency. Once you establish a system, stick to it. It might take a bit of practice, but soon, it will become second nature, and you'll spend less time tidying up and more time enjoying your clean, organized space.

Embracing these housekeeping strategies results in a clean living space. It cultivates a mindset of order and discipline that can spill over into every aspect of your life. Whether it's managing your schedule, tackling assignments, or planning your budget, the principles of simplicity, regularity, and organization are universally applicable. So, roll up your sleeves, and let's turn the chaos into harmony, one clean sweep at a time.

Laundry 101: From Sorting to Stain Removal

When doing laundry, it's easy to think it's just a matter of tossing your clothes in the machine, pouring some detergent, and hitting 'start.' However, if you've ever turned a load of whites pink or shrunk your favorite sweater to the size of a Barbie doll outfit, you know there's more to it. Let's demystify the process and turn you into a laundry wizard, or at least someone who can do their laundry without texting SOS to mom.

Sorting Laundry Like a Pro

Sorting is about more than just separating the lights from the darks. It's about preventing your vibrant red socks from staging a coup and turning everything pink. Start by dividing your laundry into categories: whites, lights, and darks. But here's a pro tip: consider fabric type and dirtiness level. Heavy items like towels and jeans deserve their own load; they require more water and have a different tumbling rhythm than t-shirts or underwear. Also, very dirty or sweaty clothes should be washed separately to avoid turning your whole load into a muddy mess.

While sorting, check the care tags—those little labels tell you everything from water temperature to drying instructions. If it says 'hand wash only,' believe it. It's not a challenge; it's a warning. Ignoring these can lead to disaster. So, respect the tags, and they'll help you keep your clothes in wearable condition.

Mastering the Wash Cycle

Choosing the proper wash cycle can be the difference between clean success and laundry disasters. Most washers have basic settings like Normal, Delicate, Heavy Duty, and Permanent Press. Normal is your go-to for everyday items, handling moderate soils with warm water and a fast spin. Delicate is best for fragile fabrics like silk or lace, offering slow agitation and a gentle spin. Heavy Duty tackles the dirtiest loads like towels and workwear, using hot water and a vigorous wash. Permanent Press is perfect for synthetic or blended fabrics, reducing wrinkles by combining warm water with a cool-down rinse.

Water temperature is crucial for both cleaning power and fabric care. Hot water works wonders for heavily soiled clothes and whites, as it sanitizes better. But beware—it can act like a fabric bully, roughing up your clothes and fading colors. Warm water is milder, making it perfect for synthetics and mixed loads. Cold water is the budget- and eco-friendly choice, ideal for darks and delicate fabrics. It helps prevent colors from bleeding and uses less energy. Choosing the right temperature will clean your clothes and help them last longer.

Effective Stain Removal

Stain removal can be tricky? Treat stains ASAP. Don't just stare in horror when you spill coffee on your shirt. Act quickly. Rinse under cold water to prevent the stain from setting. Use cold water for protein-based stains like blood or sweat, as hot water will set the stain, making it a permanent part of the item.

For a DIY stain remover, mix a tablespoon of white vinegar, a teaspoon of liquid dish soap, and a quart of warm water. Apply this solution to the stain and let it sit before laundering. This mix is especially effective on food and grass stains. For oil stains, sprinkle some baking soda on the stain, let it absorb the oil for a few hours, then brush off before washing. These simple home remedies can be surprisingly effective at tackling most stains without the need for harsh chemicals.

Caring for Delicates

Delicates are the divas of the fabric world; they need special attention. These include items like underwear, lingerie, silk shirts, and any fabric that looks at a washing machine and feels threatened. Hand washing is the best way to care for delicates. Fill a basin with cool water and a gentle detergent. Submerge the items, gently swishing them around, then rinse thoroughly and lay flat to dry. If you must use a washing machine, place them in a mesh laundry bag to protect them from the agitation and spin cycles.

Avoid the dryer as much as possible. High heat can be the nemesis of delicate fabrics. Instead, lay them flat on a towel away from direct sunlight. This prevents deformation and preserves the fabric's integrity. Treating your delicates with kid gloves can extend their life and keep them looking their best.

In essence, doing laundry properly is about respecting the fabric, understanding the care instructions, and treating stains like mini-crises that need immediate attention. With these strategies in your arsenal, you're well-equipped to confidently tackle your laundry, ensuring your clothes look their best and last longer. So, next time you sort your laundry or face a daunting stain, remember these tips, and you'll find that laundry day can be less of a chore and more of a triumph.

Basic Home Repairs: A DIY Guide

Every home requires maintenance to keep everything running smoothly. Whether it's a leaky faucet that performs its own nocturnal symphony or a creaking door like a haunted house accessory, mastering some basic DIY home repair skills can save you a lot of money and imbue you with a sense of accomplishment.

Tool Kit Essentials

First things first, you need a toolbox. The right tools are essential for home repair. Start with the basics: a screwdriver set (flathead and Phillips), a hammer, a set of pliers, an adjustable wrench, a tape measure, a spirit level, a utility knife, and a flashlight. I always have some duct tape and a set of spanners at home. These are the unsung heroes of home maintenance, ready to jump into action when the need arises. Each tool has its own role, from tightening loose screws to measuring spaces for new fixtures. Investing in good quality tools can make all the difference, ensuring they last longer and do not fail you during a crucial repair. Keep them organized in a sturdy toolbox; a chaotic collection of tools can lead to unnecessary frustration during a repair task.

Fixing Common Household Issues

Leaky faucets and creaky doors are more than just annoyances; they are cries for help from your household fixtures. Tackling a leaky faucet usually involves replacing a worn-out washer or O-ring, which is often the culprit behind the drip. Turn off the water supply, disassemble the faucet to reach the washer, replace it, and reassemble everything. It's like performing surgery, where precision and attention to detail are paramount. For creaky doors, the fix can be as simple as lubricating the hinges with WD-40 or tightening the hinge screws. Sometimes, it's the small actions that bring the most significant relief. Remember that YouTube is a great source for finding out how to fix things.

Then there's the challenge of minor wall damages—small dents or holes that seem to mysteriously appear. Spackling paste will be your best friend here. Clean the area, apply the spackle, smooth it out, and allow it to dry before sanding to make it flush with the wall. A touch of paint, and it's like the damage was never there. These repairs aren't just about aesthetics; they're about maintaining the integrity and functionality of your space.

When to DIY vs When to Call a Professional

Now, wielding a hammer doesn't make you Thor. It's crucial to know your limits. DIY can be satisfying, but overestimating your skills can lead to more significant problems. Electrical issues, major plumbing jobs, and structural work often require professional expertise. The stakes are higher, and the risks include property damage and personal safety. Especially if you are renting your property, if you try to fix something and mess it up, you could be accused of damaging property you don't own. Assess the task at hand: if it involves complex systems or you need clarification on the process, it's wise to call in the pros. Use online tutorials and home improvement books as your guide. If a task seems overwhelming or the resources advise professional intervention, heed that advice.

Safety First

Speaking of safety, let's talk about precautions. DIY home repair is not without its hazards, and a cavalier attitude can turn a simple task into a trip to the emergency room. Always wear appropriate safety gear—goggles, gloves, and sometimes a mask, especially when dealing with dusty environments or chemicals. Understand the tools you're using and respect their power. Keep your workspace clean and organized to avoid accidents, and always let someone know you're undertaking a repair task, especially if it's a significant one.

Taking on home repairs can empower you, giving you control over your environment and the satisfaction of a job well done. With the right tools, a clear understanding of your limits, and a firm adherence to safety, you can tackle most minor repairs confidently. Keeping your home in top shape ensures a comfortable living environment. So, grab your toolbox, roll up your sleeves, and let the repairs begin!

Car Maintenance: Essentials Every Young Adult Should Know

Keeping your ride in good working order is crucial if you want to avoid being stranded somewhere you would rather not be. Regular car maintenance might sound like a chore, but it's actually your secret weapon against costly repairs and unexpected breakdowns. Let's begin with the basics—oil changes and tire rotations.

Think of oil as the lifeblood of your car's engine. It keeps everything running smoothly, reducing friction and ensuring that the engine doesn't decide to go on strike. The general rule of thumb is to change the oil every 3,000 to 5,000 miles, but let's be real: who's counting miles when you're busy adulting? A better approach is to check the manufacturer's recommendations in your car's manual—that book in your glove compartment. Regular oil changes keep your engine happy and humming, and keeping up with them prevents you from the dreaded moment when your car coughs and dies mid-commute.

Now, onto tire rotations. Why bother, you ask? Well, tires are your car's shoes, and just like your sneakers would wear out unevenly if you walked with a limp, tires wear differently depending on their position in the car. Front tires carry more than half of your car's weight; thus, they tend to wear out faster. Rotating them helps extend their life, so you won't have to shell out for new tires as often. This task ensures even tire wear and maintains optimal traction on the road. It's a quick pit stop that can save you a lot of money.

Moving under the hood, let's talk about checking fluid levels—engine oil, coolant, brake fluid, and washer fluid. This is like checking your car's vital signs, ensuring everything is topped up and happy. Engine oil can be checked with the dipstick; pull it out, wipe it clean, dip it back in, and check the level. Too low? Time to top up. Coolant keeps your engine from overheating and turning your commute into a roadside barbecue. Its reservoir should be checked regularly to ensure it's between the "low" and "full" marks. Brake fluid is crucial for stopping, which is pretty essential unless you want to test your car's airbags. And washer fluid, while not critical to your car's operation, is necessary for keeping your windshield clear—because squinting through a bug-splattered windshield is no one's idea of a good time.

Understanding the hieroglyphics of dashboard warning lights can often feel like translating an ancient script. These icons are not just decorations but vital signals about your car's health. The check engine light could mean anything from a loose gas cap to something more serious like a faulty oxygen sensor. Please don't ignore it; doing so could turn a minor issue into a wallet-draining repair. Is the battery light coming on while you're driving? That's your cue to check the charging system—don't let it slide unless you want to push your car to your destination. If you see the temperature warning light, pull over because your engine is about to throw a major tantrum. Overheating can cause serious damage, so it is better to be safe than sorry.

Lastly, let's remember to prepare an emergency kit. Think of it as your car's first aid kit. Jumper cables for when your battery decides to take a nap, a tire pressure gauge to keep your tires in check, and a sturdy flashlight because, let's face it, car troubles love to happen at night on the least lit road imaginable. Throw in some essential tools, a first aid kit, and a blanket for those just-in-case moments. Being prepared might not prevent car issues, but it can make dealing with them much less stressful.

So, grab that maintenance schedule, get familiar with your car's needs, and remember, keeping your car in check is like taking care of a loyal friend—it will save you time, money, and a lot of headaches. Roll up your sleeves, and let's keep that car cruising smoothly.

Personal Safety: Awareness and Self-Defense Basics

Navigating the maze of daily life isn't just about managing chores and keeping your space tidy; it's also crucial to keep yourself safe in various situations. In this case, personal safety refers to keeping yourself safe in the physical and digital realms. Let's start with situational awareness, a skill as essential as any life-saving maneuver. It's about having your eyes wide open, not just to marvel at the world's beauty but to be aware of potential risks lurking around. Whether walking through a parking lot at night, attending a crowded event, or simply hanging out at a local café, staying alert and observant is vital. Don't walk around focused on your cell phone, oblivious to everything around you. Always scan your environment, note the exits, keep an eye on people entering or leaving, and trust your gut. If something feels off, it probably is.

Implement practices like the '10-second scan': take a quick look around every few minutes to assess your surroundings for anything unusual or potentially threatening. It's not about paranoia but preparation. This habit can make the difference between being a victim and a vigilant citizen. Also, vary your routines; predictability makes you an easier target. Switch up your travel routes, workout times, and even the places you frequent. This randomness can keep potential threats guessing and give you the upper hand.

Moving on to self-defense, it's a skill set we hope never to use but should all know—like a fire extinguisher, tucked away but ready for action. Basic self-defense starts with a strong posture and a confident presence. Attackers often target those who appear distracted or insecure. Stand tall, walk confidently, and keep your phone tucked away to stay alert. If confronted, the most effective targets are the eyes, nose, throat, and groin. Simple techniques like the palm strike (thrusting the base of your palm upward into the attacker's nose) or the knee kick can disable an attacker long enough for you to escape. Remember, the goal is not to engage but to create an opportunity to get away safely. A basic self-defense class can provide practice and build confidence, empowering you to stand your ground when necessary.

Now, let's talk about digital safety in this increasingly connected world. The Internet is a vast frontier, and while it's a place of exploration and connection, it's also rife with cyber threats. Start with the basics:

- Manage your privacy settings across all social media platforms.
- Customize who can see your posts, who can tag you, and who can share your content.
- Be wary of what you post online; personal details like your address, workplace, or even vacation plans can be used against you.
- Be on high alert for phishing attempts—those deceitful emails or messages that mimic reputable sources to steal your personal information. They often create a sense of urgency, like a problem with your bank account or a fine that needs immediate payment. Always verify the source before clicking on any links or providing personal information.

Preparing for emergencies is another essential aspect of personal safety. Imagine if a sudden natural disaster occurs or you face a dangerous situation at home or while traveling. An emergency contact list is crucial—ensure it includes not just family or friends but also local emergency numbers like the police, fire department, and medical services. Keep this list in your phone and maybe even a physical copy in your wallet; you never know when technology might fail you. Understanding basic first aid can also be a lifesaver, literally. Know how to perform CPR, treat burns, or manage bleeding. These skills are invaluable in a crisis and can make a significant difference while waiting for professional help.

By embracing these practices, you safeguard your well-being and gain a deeper sense of confidence and empowerment. Whether it's through heightened awareness, self-defense, digital safety, or emergency preparedness, these skills fortify your daily life, making you more resilient against the unexpected. So, as we continue on this journey of mastering adulting, remember that your safety is the foundation upon which all other aspects of your life are built. Remain strong, remain informed, and make safety a priority.

As we wrap up this chapter on mastering daily life tasks, remember the overarching theme: empowerment. Each skill you acquire builds your confidence and independence, from cooking and cleaning to ensuring your personal safety. These aren't just chores or tasks but stepping stones to a more capable, vibrant life. As we turn the page to the next chapter, we'll delve into the digital world, exploring how to thrive in the information age.

Notes

8
Navigating the Digital World

> *"The Internet is becoming the town square for the global village of tomorrow."*
>
> — Bill Gates

Welcome to the digital jungle! It's wild and vast, and if you're not careful, you can easily get lost among the endless tweets, posts, and content streams. In this digital age, your online presence can be as vivid and real as your physical one. You need to be aware of your digital footprint—the tracks you leave with every click, like, and share. Understanding and managing this can help you avoid the Internet's pitfalls and move towards crafting an online persona aligned with your real-world self.

Managing Your Digital Footprint: Privacy and Safety Online

Understanding Digital Footprints

Everything you do online—every post you like, every tweet you retweet, every item you browse—leaves invisible marks, like footprints in digital sand. These footprints accumulate to form your digital footprint, a comprehensive record of your online activity. This virtual trail can tell a vivid story about who you are, your likes, dislikes, habits, and even your location at any given time. While this might sound like the start of a sci-fi thriller, it's the reality of our interconnected lives. These footprints are accessible to your friends and family and potentially to employers, marketers, and predators. Thus, managing your digital footprint isn't just about privacy; it's about controlling your perception of the vast digital cosmos.

Privacy Settings and Online Behavior

Learn how to use the settings menu on social media platforms because these can significantly impact your digital privacy. Major platforms like Facebook, Instagram, and Twitter all offer customizable privacy settings that allow you to manage who sees your posts, who can tag you, and even who can comment on your activities. Adjust these settings to suit your comfort level—keep your profiles private if you don't want the entire digital world peeking into your life.

Your online behavior plays a crucial role in safeguarding your privacy. Be mindful of what you share. Posting pictures of every moment, check-ins at every location, or sharing sensitive personal information like your address or phone number can make you a target. It's like leaving your diary open in a crowded café—maybe nothing will happen, but do you really want to take that chance? Remember, the more you share, the more you expose yourself to potential risks. It's important to be cautious and responsible in your online activities.

Preventing Identity Theft

In the digital world, your personal information is as good as gold. Identity theft is a real and growing threat, where hackers can use details like your full name, date of birth, or even your pet's name (thanks to those seemingly innocent social media quizzes) to breach accounts or create new ones in your name. Protect yourself by using a password manager to generate and store complex passwords. Change these regularly, and enable two-factor authentication for an added layer of security. Remember, in the cyber world, a strong password is like a good lock on the door—it won't stop the most determined thieves but will deter the vast majority.

Cleaning Up Digital Footprints

Have you ever googled yourself? Try it, and you might be surprised at what you find. Old social media profiles, forum posts from years ago, or that blog you started and abandoned in a week are all out there, forming part of your digital footprint. Cleaning this up can be as liberating as decluttering your home. Start by deleting old accounts you no longer use. Review your privacy settings on existing profiles and remove old posts that might not reflect who you are now.

Consider this digital cleanup a necessary part of maintaining your online health, similar to how you might diet or exercise to keep your physical self in shape. It helps present a cleaner, more polished image of you to the world. Let's be honest; it can also be pretty satisfying to shed some of that digital weight.

Navigating the digital world can be challenging, but with the proper knowledge and tools, you can manage your digital footprint to safeguard your online presence. It's about being aware, cautious, and occasionally doing a bit of digital housekeeping.

Social Media Smarts: Building Your Brand Positively

In the sprawling digital playground of social media, crafting a personal brand is like building a sandcastle at the beach: you want it to stand out and withstand the waves, not get washed away with the tide. The key to a resilient digital presence lies in the foundations you lay and the materials you use. Think of your posts, shares, and comments as the building blocks of your online persona. You must understand that every tweet, Instagram story, and Facebook post contributes to your digital self-portrait. Maintaining a positive and engaging online brand can inspire and motivate your audience.

Crafting this online persona starts with aligning your social media presence with your personal and professional interests. Begin by auditing your existing profiles. Are they a true reflection of your passions and pursuits? If not, it might be time for a digital makeover. Be bold, take control, and make changes that better reflect who you are. Update your bio sections to highlight your interests, professional skills, and achievements. Use a profile picture that is both friendly and professional—a welcoming smile can go a long way! Consistently share content that resonates with your areas of interest or expertise. This authenticity makes your social media profiles more engaging. It attracts a like-minded audience, building a community around shared interests.

Now, onto networking, which, in the digital age, can often begin with a simple click. Social media platforms are teeming with opportunities to connect with industry leaders, potential mentors, and peers who share your professional interests. Engage actively but thoughtfully with their content. Comment with insightful observations, share their work while adding your own take, and don't hesitate to reach out with a well-crafted message. Remember, the goal is to foster genuine connections, not just add names to your contact list. Over time, these digital interactions can translate into collaborations, job opportunities, and lasting professional relationships.

Balancing what you share and maintaining privacy online can often feel like walking a tightrope. On one hand, engaging actively with your community can lead to greater visibility and more opportunities. On the other, oversharing can make you vulnerable to privacy breaches and online fatigue. Strike a balance by setting clear boundaries about what aspects of your life are open for public viewing. Use privacy settings to control who sees your posts, and think twice before sharing location details or overly personal information. Just as you wouldn't hand out copies of your house key to strangers, only hand out access to your personal life if you're comfortable with the audience.

Handling online conflict constructively is another critical skill in maintaining a positive digital presence. Hiding behind anonymity can sometimes lead to heated exchanges and hurtful comments. When faced with online negativity, take a step back and assess whether the comment warrants a response. If you choose to engage, aim to de-escalate the situation with calm, reasoned responses or agree to disagree respectfully. Don't hesitate to use the block and report functions if the conversation turns abusive. Your digital space is your domain; you have every right to keep it positive and healthy.

Navigating social media wisely involves:

- Building a positive presence that reflects your true self
- Networking effectively
- Sharing prudently
- Managing conflicts with grace

These strategies can help you maintain positivity in your social media accounts and remain open to opportunities, making every digital interaction meaningful.

Understanding Global Issues: Becoming a Global Citizen

The world is a big place, yet, thanks to the Internet and global communication, it feels like we're all neighbors. With this closeness comes a greater awareness of the massive global challenges—issues like climate change that respect no borders and social inequalities that are as old as time yet as current as today's headlines. When confronted with these issues, it's easy to feel like a tiny cog in a vast machine. However, even the smallest cog can make the gears turn differently.

Global awareness isn't just about knowing these issues exist; it's about understanding how they affect people and places far from your backyard. Take climate change, for example. It's not just about polar bears on melting ice caps; it's also about farmers in your region grappling with unpredictable weather patterns and many nations facing severe threats from rising sea levels. Then there's social inequality, a many-headed monster that manifests in poverty, lack of education, and limited healthcare access, compounded by systemic racism and gender discrimination across the globe. Recognizing the interconnectedness of these issues is the first step towards becoming a part of the solution.

Let's talk about cultural sensitivity and appreciation. In this global village, every tweet you send, every meme you share, and every comment you make can travel around the world in a heartbeat. This digital era calls for a new kind of literacy—cultural sensitivity, where understanding the context of different cultures can help you navigate the global conversations occurring every second. Cultural sensitivity requires an understanding that what's considered humorous or harmless in one culture might be deeply offensive in another. It's about respecting and approaching these differences with a learning mindset rather than judgment.

Whether you're interacting online or backpacking across continents, the ability to appreciate and respect other cultures enriches your experiences and broadens your worldview.

Contributing to solutions for these global issues might seem daunting, but it's possible. Every significant movement starts with individual actions. Volunteering, for instance, isn't just about giving up a Saturday afternoon to plant trees or clean up beaches, though those are a good place to start. It's also about lending your voice and platform to advocate for policies addressing these issues. Join or initiate campaigns that promote renewable energy, support education for underprivileged children, or fight for equal rights for all. Your involvement can also be as simple as making lifestyle changes—reducing waste, supporting ethical businesses, or educating yourself and others about these issues. Each action might be a drop in the ocean, but together, they create waves of change that can reshape our world.

It is essential to remain informed but choose quality over quantity when it comes to the news you consume. Follow reputable news outlets, subscribe to journals offering in-depth analyses of global issues, and use technology to your advantage by setting up alerts for passionate topics. Rather than passively consuming this information, engage with it. Discuss it in forums, share it within your networks, and even blog about your thoughts and learnings. Continuous learning is crucial—not just in understanding the issues but in keeping your knowledge current in a world that changes by the nanosecond.

Understanding the complexities of global issues requires awareness, action, empathy, and an unyielding commitment to learning and understanding more about the world and the people who share it with you. As you forge ahead, remember that as a global citizen, you are responsible for making the world a better place, more informed, compassionate, and culturally sensitive.

Traveling Smart: Tips for Safe and Budget-Friendly Adventures

Traveling is an adventure that offers an array of experiences, each more enriching and enlightening than the last. However, every adventure requires strategic planning and an affordable budget. Effective planning and budgeting ensure that your travels are memorable for the right reasons, not for running out of money midway through your journey.

Planning your trip requires a mix of excitement and meticulous detail. Start by defining your travel goals: are you chasing the Northern Lights in Iceland, backpacking across Southeast Asia, or exploring the ancient ruins of Rome? Each destination has its own set of expenses and logistical considerations. Create a budget early on, accounting for the big-ticket items like flights and accommodation and daily expenses such as food, local transport, and entrance fees to attractions. Tools like travel budget apps or spreadsheets can be invaluable, helping you keep track of expenses and adjust in real-time.

Finding deals is part art, part science. Early booking can secure the best prices, especially for flights and hotels.

Consider traveling during the off-season; you'll save money and avoid the tourist crowds, allowing for a more authentic experience. Websites and apps dedicated to travel deals are worth exploring—sign up for alerts from sites like Skyscanner or Scott's Cheap Flights, and you might snag a deal that cuts your flight costs in half. Accommodation can also be a flexible field in your budget—options like hostels, vacation rentals, or even house-sitting can offer immersive experiences at a fraction of the cost of traditional hotels.

Travel safety is your passport to a smooth adventure. Research your destination ahead of time—not just the best beaches or must-see landmarks, but also the practical aspects; for example, what are the typical tourist scams? How safe is public transport? Is the tap water drinkable? Knowledge is power; in this case, it's the power to avoid pitfalls. Keep digital copies of important documents like your passport and insurance—cloud storage can be a lifesaver if physical copies are lost or stolen. A minimalist approach to your luggage eases your load and reduces the risk of theft. A sturdy, lockable backpack and the use of hotel safes can keep your valuables secure while you explore.

Respecting cultural norms and etiquette during your travels shows respect and earns respect. This can range from dressing conservatively in religious sites to learning a few basic phrases in the local language and understanding local customs. Each gesture of respect opens doors to deeper interactions and richer experiences.

Sustainable travel practices are your contribution to ensuring the beauty of destinations remains for generations to come.

This means considering the environmental and social impacts of your travel choices. Opt for public transport, biking, or walking rather than renting a car. Support local economies by eating at local restaurants and buying from artisans and local markets instead of chain stores. Be conscious of your environmental footprint—simple actions like carrying a reusable water bottle, avoiding single-use plastics, and choosing eco-friendly tours and accommodations can make a significant difference. Engaging in sustainable travel practices can set a trend that encourages others to follow suit, ensuring that the destinations we love remain vibrant and vital.

Navigating the nuances of smart travel—from budgeting and safety to cultural etiquette and sustainability—is an art that enriches your travel experience, making it safer, more affordable, and more respectful of the incredible places you visit. With these strategies, you're well-equipped to embark on your adventures confidently, ready to explore the world and leave it a little better than you found it.

Volunteering: Giving Back and Gaining Experience

Imagine stepping into a world where every action you take radiates ripples that touch lives, where each hour you dedicate helps paint a larger picture of change and positivity. This isn't just fantasy—it's the profound reality of volunteering. Whether you're planting trees, mentoring youth, or serving meals at a local shelter, volunteering isn't just about giving back; it's a two-way street that offers profound benefits for the communities you help and your personal and professional growth.

Finding the right volunteer opportunities can sometimes feel like finding a needle in a haystack, especially if you're looking to align these opportunities with your interests and values. Start local—community centers, religious organizations, and schools are often looking for volunteers. They can provide opportunities that might not be listed on larger platforms. For a broader scope, websites like VolunteerMatch, Idealist, or even LinkedIn can offer many options, ranging from local community projects to virtual volunteering opportunities that allow you to contribute from the comfort of your home. When choosing a volunteer spot, consider what skills you can offer and what skills you might want to develop. Are you a budding graphic designer eager to practice your skills? Look for nonprofits in need of marketing support. Passionate about education? Tutoring or mentoring could be immensely fulfilling and impactful.

The benefits of volunteering extend far beyond the immediate impact of the tasks you perform. On a personal level, it's a powerful way to build empathy and understanding, connecting you with people and circumstances that might be far removed from your everyday life. It's an eye-opener and a heart-opener, showing you different slices of life and helping cultivate gratitude and perspective. Professionally, volunteering can be just as advantageous. It's a chance to develop new skills—leadership, communication, problem-solving, and teamwork, to name a few—that apply to virtually any career. Plus, it bolsters your resume, demonstrating to potential employers that you can take the initiative and commit to making a positive impact. Networking is another significant benefit; you meet people from all walks of life, including potential mentors, friends, and even future employers.

For those with wanderlust, international volunteering opens a whole new dimension of giving back. It allows you to immerse yourself in a new culture while contributing to projects that can profoundly impact local communities. However, this type of volunteering requires thorough preparation and consideration. Cultural sensitivity is paramount; take the time to learn about the customs, language, and expectations of the place you're visiting to ensure your presence is respectful and beneficial. Logistically, international volunteering often requires planning—visas, vaccinations, and potentially complex travel arrangements. Organizations like the Peace Corps and international NGOs provide structured opportunities but always perform diligent research to find programs that have a tangible, positive impact on the communities they aim to help.

Making a lasting impact through volunteering isn't about the grand gestures but the sustained, thoughtful contributions that accumulate over time. Consistency is key. Commit to a long-term project or a recurring volunteer role if you can. This not only gives you the chance to see the ongoing impacts of your efforts but also allows you to build stronger relationships within the community you're serving. Beyond your individual effort, think about how to amplify the benefits—can you recruit friends or coworkers to join the cause or use your social media platform to raise awareness and support? Sometimes, the most impactful action is inspiring others to join in.

Volunteering is a vibrant pathway lined with opportunities for growth, learning, and connection. It's about knitting your skills and energy into the larger community and global well-being fabric. Whether it's through teaching, building, healing, or creating, every volunteer effort carves out a space where hope can flourish and communities can thrive.

Continuous Learning: Keeping Skills Updated in a Rapidly Changing World

Committing to continuous learning is essential to remaining updated, enhancing your skills, and developing sufficient flexibility to adapt to new information in the modern world.

Lifelong Learning Mindset

The most successful professionals perceive learning as a lifelong marathon rather than a sprint to a diploma. This mindset is about being curious and proactive, seeing every challenge as a chance to grow and every failure as a lesson learned. It's about keeping your brain active with new skills and knowledge. Adopting this mindset means viewing every day as an opportunity to learn something new, whether it's a better way to manage your time or a new tech tool that could revolutionize your workflow.

Online Learning Platforms

In an age where information is just a click away, online learning platforms are like your digital libraries, brimming with knowledge on just about anything you could wish to learn. Platforms such as Coursera, Udemy, and Khan Academy offer courses on everything from quantum physics to digital marketing, many created by top universities and companies. Then there's LinkedIn Learning, which provides bite-sized courses tailored to enhance professional skills. These platforms offer flexibility, allowing you to learn at your own pace, on your own schedule, and in your own space. It's like having a personal tutor available 24/7, ready to help you beef up your CV or master a new hobby.

Keeping Up with Industry Trends

Staying informed is crucial as industries constantly evolve. To stay on the cutting edge of your field, you need to keep abreast of changes by regularly reading industry journals, subscribing to relevant podcasts, and following thought leaders on social media. Attend webinars and virtual conferences whenever possible. These resources keep you updated on current trends and provide insight into where the industry is headed, allowing you to anticipate rather than react to changes.

Learning from Experience

Lastly, always appreciate the power of old-fashioned Experience. Every job you perform, every project you undertake, and every interaction you have is a learning opportunity. Reflect on these experiences. What went well? What could have gone better? How will you approach similar tasks in the future? This reflective practice turns everyday experiences into valuable lessons that no classroom or online course can fully replicate. Moreover, interacting with diverse groups of people, whether in your community or workplace, can provide new perspectives and insights that challenge your thinking and promote personal and professional growth.

Remain agile, adaptable, and always tuned into the frequencies of change. By committing to lifelong learning, you ensure that no matter where your career or personal interests take you, you'll be ready to meet the challenges head-on, equipped with the requisite knowledge.

Embrace the transformative power of lifelong learning. It keeps your skills sharp and enriches your life, fuels innovation, and builds connections that transcend geographical and digital boundaries. With knowledge and a commitment to continuous learning, you're ready to adapt to and shape the future.

Notes

Keeping the Game Alive

"You have not lived today until you have done something for someone who can never repay you."

— John Bunyan

Hello, incredible reader!

Congratulations on finishing Life Skills for Young Adults! You've taken a powerful step toward creating the life you deserve—one filled with financial security, emotional resilience, and career success. But before we part ways, I have one last favor to ask of you.

Now that you've gained the tools to conquer life's challenges, it's time to pass the torch. By leaving your honest review on Amazon, you'll show other young adults where to find the same help that made a difference in your life.

Your review is more than just words—it's a guiding light for someone searching for answers. Imagine another young adult, much like you, standing at the crossroads, unsure of their next move. With your review, you're not only sharing your thoughts but offering them the chance to transform their future.

Your review can help ...

- One more person discovers how to take control of their finances.

- One more dreamer finds the courage to chase their goals.
- One more young adult builds the resilience to overcome life's hurdles.
- One more future leader unlocks their full potential.

Together, we can keep Life Skills for Young Adults alive—by passing on knowledge, encouragement, and hope.

It only takes a moment to make a big impact.

>>>Click here to leave your review on Amazon.

Thank you for being part of this journey. Your willingness to give back ensures that the knowledge in this book continues to inspire and empower young adults everywhere.

Here's to your continued success and to the lives you'll change by sharing your voice.

With gratitude,

SquareRoets

P.S. Knowledge grows when it's shared. Know someone who could benefit from this book? Share it with them and help us keep the game alive!

Conclusion

"The only limit to our realization of tomorrow will be our doubts of today."

— Franklin D. Roosevelt

Well, here we are at the end of our grand tour through the bustling metropolis of adulthood. It's been quite the journey, hasn't it? From mastering the art of budgeting to understanding the emotional rollercoaster that is your late teens and early twenties, we've covered a lot of ground. Let's take a moment to consider all the tools you now have in your kit.

This guide isn't just a collection of life hacks; it's a comprehensive handbook for navigating independence. We covered everything from financial literacy and emotional resilience to career-building and basic cooking skills. This guide is designed to help you survive and thrive in young adulthood.

Remember when we first started? You might have felt unsure about "adulting," but now, you're ready to budget like a pro, manage emotions like a Zen master, and confidently tackle your career. This guide has been your training; now you're ready to take on the world. Appreciate how far you've come and the skills you've mastered.

From setting SMART financial goals to practicing mindfulness, from effective communication in relationships to managing your digital footprint, these aren't just lessons; they're your toolkit for building your dream life. Each part of this guide is a stepping stone towards greater confidence and capability.

If there's one takeaway, it's that learning never ends. Life is a continuous journey of discovery, and every challenge is a lesson. The skills we've discussed are just the start—keep building, growing, and pushing your limits. Your future holds endless possibilities for growth. Embrace this journey with enthusiasm and let it inspire you to keep learning and growing.

Now, it's your turn to put these tools to use. Apply budgeting next time you check your bank account, use conflict resolution in your next debate, and practice mindfulness during your daily commute. Real change comes from action—so dive in, make mistakes, learn, and grow. You have the power to shape your life and make it what you want it to be.

As you grow, remember to help others. Share your knowledge, mentor, and guide those just starting out. Each one, teach one—right? Your journey inspires and lights the way for others.

Adulthood has its bumps—potholes, detours, and flat tires—but with the right skills and mindset, you can handle them. You're ready and not alone. Remember, it's OK to stumble. It's OK to feel lost at times. What's important is that you keep going, and we're here to support you every step of the way.

As we wrap up, I hope this guide becomes more than a manual— it's your companion on this exciting journey. My wish for you is not just success in the conventional sense but a life filled with learning, growth, and happiness. Here's to your journey, adventures, and stories you'll create. The best is yet to come!

Safe travels, young explorer. May your path be bright and your adventures grand.

Notes

References

Omololu, E. (2024, June 3). 10 essential money tips for young adults. *Forbes.* https://www.forbes.com/sites/enochomololu/2023/09/18/10-essential-money-tips-for-young-adults/

Team, I. (2024, February 28). *What is a credit score? Definition, factors, and ways to raise it.* Investopedia. https://www.investopedia.com/terms/c/credit_score.asp

Hannahallton. (2024, February 9). *Best Savings Strategies for Short-Term and Long-Term Goals - PlainsCapital Bank.* PlainsCapital Bank. https://www.plainscapital.com/blog/best-savings-strategies-for-short-term-and-long-term-goals/

Hannahallton. (2024, February 9). *Best Savings Strategies for Short-Term and Long-Term Goals - PlainsCapital Bank.* PlainsCapital Bank. https://www.plainscapital.com/blog/best-savings-strategies-for-short-term-and-long-term-goals/

Cfa, B. B. (2024, January 31). *How to invest in your 20s: 7 tips to get started.* Bankrate. https://www.bankrate.com/investing/best-ways-to-get-into-investing-in-your-20s/

Indeed Editorial Team. (2024, May 28). *How to start a side hustle in 7 steps (Including examples).* Indeed Career Guide. https://ca.indeed.com/career-advice/finding-a-job/how-to-start-side-hustle

Alpaio, K. (2024, February 9). *How to negotiate your starting salary.* Harvard Business Review. https://hbr.org/2022/07/how-to-negotiate-your-starting-salary

Health care coverage options for young adults. (n.d.). HealthCare.gov. https://www.healthcare.gov/young-adults/

Richmond, S. (2023, December 19). *Why save for retirement in your 20s?* Investopedia. https://www.investopedia.com/articles/personal-finance/040315/why-save-retirement-your-20s.asp

Staff, N. A. (2024, May 28). Teen Stress: 10 Stress-Management Skills for Teenagers. *Newport Academy.* https://www.newportacademy.com/resources/mental-health/teen-stress-relief/

Thomas Jefferson University and Jefferson Health. (2024, March 19). Mindfulness for anxiety: just as effective as medication. *Jefferson Health.*

https://www.jeffersonhealth.org/your-health/living-well/mindfulness-for-anxiety-just-as-effective-as-medication

Jesse. (2024, February 1). *Empowering Teens to Triumph Over Fear of Failure: A Parent's Guide*. theattitudeadvantage.com. https://theattitudeadvantage.com/all-posts/empowering-teens-to-triumph-over-fear-of-failure-a-parents-guide-2/

Valkenburg, P., Beyens, I., Pouwels, J. L., Van Driel, I. I., & Keijsers, L. (2021). Social Media Use and Adolescents' Self-Esteem: Heading for a Person-Specific Media Effects Paradigm. *Journal of Communication*, 71(1), 56–78. https://doi.org/10.1093/joc/jqaa039

Lmft, M. H. (2024, April 22). *Active listening: a key to deeper intimacy and understanding in your relationship*. Holding Hope Marriage and Family Therapy. https://holdinghopemft.com/active-listening-a-key-to-deeper-intimacy-and-understanding-in-your-relationship/

Smith, M., MA. (2024, February 5). *Setting healthy boundaries in relationships*. HelpGuide.org. https://www.helpguide.org/articles/relationships-communication/setting-healthy-boundaries-in-relationships.htm

Youth Conflict Resolution Techniques + Life Skills: Processing Conflict During a Crisis. (n.d.). https://elcentronc.org/advocacy/youth-conflict-resolution-techniques-life-skills-processing-conflict-during-a-crisis/

Madden, T. (2024, February 20). How to build and maintain professional relationships. *Forbes*. https://www.forbes.com/sites/forbescoachescouncil/2023/02/02/how-to-build-and-maintain-professional-relationships/

Monster.com. (2024, April 26). *11 of the Best Free Career Aptitude Tests*. https://www.monster.com/career-advice/article/best-free-career-assessment-tools

Informational Interviews - Career engagement. (2023, October 6). Career Engagement. https://career.berkeley.edu/start-exploring/informational-interviews/

3 tips to maximize a summer internship. (2023, January 23). Harvard FAS | Mignone Center for Career Success. https://careerservices.fas.harvard.edu/classes/3-tips-to-maximize-a-summer-internship/

Workassist. (2023, April 15). *Crafting an effective resume and cover letter*. https://www.linkedin.com/pulse/crafting-effective-resume-cover-letter-workassist-in

Generation, E. N. (2023, September 11). *The Most In-Demand Digital Skills for 2023 and beyond*. https://www.linkedin.com/pulse/most-in-demand-digital-skills-2023-beyond-elementsnextgeneration

References

CAKE.com Inc. (n.d.). *26 Most effective time management techniques — Clockify*. Clockify. https://clockify.me/time-management-techniques

Urquijo, I., Extremera, N., & Azanza, G. (2019). The contribution of emotional intelligence to career success: Beyond personality traits. *International Journal of Environmental Research and Public Health/International Journal of Environmental Research and Public Health*, 16(23), 4809. https://doi.org/10.3390/ijerph16234809

Jeffrey, S. (2024, April 16). 12 Powerful Creative Problem-Solving techniques that work. *Scott Jeffrey*. https://scottjeffrey.com/creative-problem-solving-techniques/

Rd, B. L. K. M. (2024, January 25). I Set My Grocery Budget to $50 for the Week—Here's How I Made It Work. *Allrecipes*. https://www.allrecipes.com/50-dollar-grocery-budget-and-dinners-for-one-week-8549649

Hubbard, A. (2022, September 23). *18 easy and green DIY recipes to clean all the things, plus health benefits*. Healthline. https://www.healthline.com/health/easy-green-diy-recipes-to-clean-all-the-things-plus-health-benefits

Stanley, J. (2024, March 13). 98 home repairs you don't need to call a pro for. *Family Handyman*. https://www.familyhandyman.com/list/home-repairs-you-can-do-yourself/

Travelers. (2023, February 20). *8 important car maintenance services teens and new drivers need to know*. https://www.travelers.com/resources/auto/maintenance/8-important-car-maintenance-services-teens-need-to-know

Bouchrika, I. (2024, June 10). *How to manage your digital footprint in 2024: 20 tips for students*. Research.com. https://research.com/education/how-to-manage-digital-footprint

Burger, E. (2024, March 26). Career Development: How volunteering can Create opportunity. *VolunteerHub*. https://volunteerhub.com/blog/career-development-volunteerism

Duffy, J. (2024, March 1). *The best online learning services for 2024*. PCMAG. https://www.pcmag.com/picks/best-online-learning-services?test_uuid=05GCyCmbxBRLzxn0Zys1DBH&test_variant=b

Jacobs, K. (2020, February 3). *Quick travel tips for the young adult on a limited budget*. https://www.myautoloan.com/ . Retrieved July 7, 2024, from https://www.myautoloan.com/content-articles/quick-travel-tips-for-the-young-adult-on-a-limited-budget.html

Notes

Notes

Printed in Great Britain
by Amazon